Sadat and His Legacy

EGYPT AND THE WORLD, 1977–1997

On the Occasion of the Twentieth Anniversary
of President Sadat's Journey to Jerusalem

Contributors:

Eliahu Ben Elissar
Wat Cluverius
Hermann Frederick Eilts
Ahmed Fakhr
Saad Eddin Ibrahim
Martin Indyk
Samuel Lewis
Ahmed Maher el-Sayed
Robert Pelletreau

Kenneth Pollack
Peter Rodman
Camelia Anwar Sadat
Abdel Monem Said
Robert Satloff
Shimon Shamir
Kenneth Stein
Shibley Telhami
Ehud Ya'ari

Edited with introduction
by Jon B. Alterman

THE WASHINGTON INSTITUTE
FOR NEAR EAST POLICY

A Washington Institute Monograph

© 1998 by the Washington Institute for Near East Policy

Published in 1998 in the United States of America by the Washington Institute for Near East Policy, 1828 L Street N.W. Suite 1050, Washington, DC 20036

Library of Congress Cataloging-in-Publication Data

Alterman, Jon B., 1964-
     Sadat and his legacy / Egypt and the world, 1977–1997 : on the occasion of the twentieth anniversary of President Sadat's journey to Jerusalem / contributors, Eliahu Ben-Elissar ... [et al.] ; edited with introduction by Jon B. Alterman.
     p. cm.
     A collection of papers presented at an international conference, held November 13–14, 1997, and sponsored by the Washington Institute for Near East Policy.
     Includes bibliographical references.
     ISBN 0-944029-74-4
     1. Sadat, Anwar, 1918- —Contributions in diplomacy—Congresses. 2. Egypt—Politics and government—Congresses. 3. Egypt—Foreign relations—Israel—Congresses. 4. Israel—Foreign relations—Egypt—Congresses. 5. Arab–Israeli conflict—1993- —Peace—Congresses. I. Ben Elissar, Eliahu. II. Alterman, Jon B., 1964– . III. Washington Institute for Near East Policy.
DT107.85.S375 1998   98-14803
962.05'4'092—dc21   CIP

Cover design by Naylor Design Inc.
Photos: UPI/Corbis–Bettmann Archives

Contents

iii

iv

Preface

Few moments in the history of the Middle East were as
dramatic as President Anwar Sadat's descending from
his airplane and stepping, for the first time, on Israeli
soil. In a breathtaking gesture of goodwill, he broke
through the mistrust and animosity of three decades of
war and made real the prospect of peace, Israel's long-
sought goal. Although full peace between Arabs and
Israelis has not come as quickly as Sadat and his partner,
Menachem Begin, had hoped, the example of Sadat's
courageous journey—and Israel's warm welcome to its
wartime foe— remains the standard by which all future
peacemaking efforts will be judged.

In November 1997, The Washington Institute was
proud to convene a special conference to commemorate
the twentieth anniversary of President Sadat's journey to
Jerusalem. Numerous scholars, diplomats, journalists,
government officials, and even the late president's
daughter, Camelia, gathered in Washington for two days
of reminiscences, analysis, and discussion about Sadat
the man, his strategy at home and abroad, and his legacy
for Egypt and the wider Middle East. While a
celebration of Sadat and his hopes for peace, the
conference was, in retrospect, a bittersweet event;
convened against the backdrop of Egypt's refusal to
attend the Doha economic conference and the deepening
impasse in the Israeli–Palestinian peace process, it
underscored how much of Sadat's vision—both for
Egypt's bilateral peace with Israel and for the wider
search for comprehensive peace—remains unfulfilled.
Indeed, many attendees were wistful that the Middle
East today has so few leaders of the stature of Sadat and

v

Begin, farsighted statesmen able to see the future and build it one day at a time.

This volume includes the oral presentations from that conference and the discussions that followed. Edited by Jon B. Alterman, a 1997–98 Soref research fellow at the Institute, who also wrote an original introduction for this book, these presentations provide both a guide to the past and, to a surprising degree, a way of thinking about the future.

Mike Stein	Barbi Weinberg
President	Chairman

Introduction

By Jon B. Alterman

Anwar Sadat remains a controversial figure in the Middle East. Praised as a prophet and cursed as a traitor, neither his death in 1981 nor the passage of time have resolved the ongoing debate about the man and his legacy. There is not yet an authoritative biography of Sadat in either Arabic or English, although Sadat himself made several efforts during his career to define himself to the Egyptian public and the world community.[1]

Some of the controversy over Sadat arises from the fact that the future that Sadat predicted has not yet come to pass. Egypt's economy, while showing encouraging signs of life, has not yet produced prosperity for a large number of its citizens. Peace with Israel, although secure on the Egyptian border, has left the Palestinians with fewer fruits of peace than they and the Egyptians had hoped they would have. Many who have lived through the unfulfilled promises of Sadat's vision have continued to speak and act violently against his legacy.

For many, Sadat's legacy is a series of ongoing processes—the Arab–Israeli peace process, Egyptian economic development, and political liberalization, among others—and this surely has something to do with continuing debates over his legacy. Those with a stake in

---

[1] Most notably, *Revolt on the Nile* (New York: John Day, 1957) and *In Search of Identity* (New York: Harper and Row, 1978). Part of the problem may lie in irreconcilable inconsistencies between the two accounts. See David Hirst and Irene Beeson, *Sadat* (London: Faber and Faber, 1981), p. 59.

current issues speak about Sadat as a coded way to criticize current leaders and influence current developments. In Egypt in particular, debates purportedly over Sadat have served as cover for discussions about economic change, corruption, political repression, international politics, and negotiating strategy in the peace process.

The foregoing, however, is insufficient to explain the relative unease that historians and other students of the region have in finding a place for Sadat. The fact is that there remains a tension about Sadat, an inability to explain a man who appeared equally comfortable with peasants and presidents, a man who seemed at home with a feisty international press corps yet who imprisoned thousands of his domestic political opponents.

Much of this discomfort springs from Sadat's own interest in presenting himself as a statesman and world leader. Although he certainly was that, he derived his place on the world stage from his success in and knowledge of the Egyptian scene. It was in Egyptian domestic politics that Sadat learned his exquisite sense of timing, and in that same setting that he learned the importance of the dramatic gesture. It was on the Egyptian political stage that Sadat learned to create photo opportunities, and on that same stage that he learned how to build public support without the vindication of contested elections.

Most important, it was on the Egyptian stage that Anwar Sadat learned how to gain trust. He did so not by demonstrations of overwhelming force, nor by blackmailing his interlocutors with damaging information. He did so through a blend of humility and hauteur, a willingness to be underestimated, and an understanding of the importance of building confidence, step by step, with one's adversaries. Sadat used all of these skills to implement his vision for Egypt. His vision was not borne out of bureaucratic planning or academic strategizing, nor was it laden with detail. It was a visceral vision that wedded Sadat's deeply held Egyptian nationalism and his political sense of the realistic possibilities for Egypt's future. It is only through understanding Sadat in his Egyptian context that his legacy can be assessed.

Anwar Sadat's political ascendance began with his matriculation in the military academy. Previously reserved for the scions of elite and noble families, the academy opened its doors to the Egyptian middle class in May 1936.[2] The effect was to bring together in the military the very groups that were most politically active in Egypt and most eager for a change in the status quo. These sons of clerks, low-ranking officers, and small businessmen brought into the officer corps the political ferment then present on the streets of Cairo. In the years after he entered the academy, Sadat was active in many political movements, including the Muslim Brotherhood, the fascist Young Egypt, the pro-palace Iron Guard, and a secret military group called the Free Officers, which sought to liberate Egypt from British influence. He spent much of World War II in jail for aiding Germany in its

---

[2]   The ruling Wafd party opened the academy's doors wider in a nationalist move against the British. Of the eleven founding members of the Free Officers movement, eight entered the academy in its first year of more open admissions, two in the second year, and one in the third. See the table in P. J. Vatikiotis, *The Egyptian Army in Politics* (Bloomington: Indiana University Press, 1961), pp. 48–49.

efforts to force the British from Egypt. Upon his release, he resumed his political activities and emerged as part of the "inner circle" when the Free Officers overthrew the monarchy in a coup on July 23, 1952. As a group, the Free Officers were largely unknown to the Egyptian public for months after the coup. Sadat was in no way visible among them at first, but as time passed he took on a public role as a fiery and voluble propagandist of the revolution. He was named editor of *al-Gumhuriya*, the daily paper established as a regime mouthpiece in 1953, and in its pages he became an outspoken opponent of Western imperialism. Sadat also authored a number of books in the late 1950s explaining the revolution to the Egyptian public, and he took on leadership roles in government-sponsored mass political organizations.

As factional politics swirled within the leadership of the Free Officers, from the purge of Gen. Muhammad Naguib and Col. Khalid Mohieddin in 1954 to the dismissal of the military leadership after the 1967 debacle, Sadat appeared detached from the action. Insulting caricatures of him appeared in the press, and jokes circulated about the lack of esteem he enjoyed among his colleagues. Although he was named speaker of the National Assembly in 1959 and vice president in 1969, few took him as a serious contender for power. When Gamal Abdel Nasser died and Sadat ascended to the presidency in October 1970, Department of State officers responsible for the Middle East knew almost nothing about this eighteen-year veteran of Egyptian cabinet politics, and it has been widely reported that the Central Intelligence Agency estimated he would last no longer than six months in office before a "stronger" leader emerged.

Sadat's unassuming nature may have been partly by design. In *Search for Identity*, Sadat mentions that while in prison he read an article on psychology in *Reader's Digest* that changed his life.[3] His professing a taste for what many would consider pedestrian reading material contrasts sharply with his predecessor, whose book *Philosophy of the Revolution* drops the name of a Luigi Pirandello play that Nasser later admitted he had never read.[4] Sadat's refusal to portray himself as an intellectual, as a power broker, or as a schemer surely kept him from becoming a lightning rod for political opponents, although it also subjected him to occasional ridicule and disrespect. The extent to which Sadat consciously and strategically ensured that he was underestimated will never be known, although he benefited from this assessment time after time.

Upon coming to power, Sadat acted quickly to secure his rule. He moved strongly against Ali Sabri and other leaders seeking to use the mass political party, the Arab Socialist Union, as an alternative center of leadership. Understanding that the Soviet Union supported the Sabri faction, Sadat turned to the U.S. government for support, making an extraordinary yet secret appeal for friendship in May 1971 to Secretary of State William Rogers on the latter's trip through the region. Although Egypt and the United States did not enjoy diplomatic relations, Sadat offered to jettison Egypt's fifteen-year alliance with the Soviet Union in favor of an American arrangement. U.S. officials, who

---

3   *Search for Identity*, p. 76.
4   The play is "Six Characters in Search of an Author." See Kennett Love, *Suez: The Twice-Fought War* (New York: McGraw-Hill, 1969), p. 411.

knew little of Sadat to begin with, had no idea whether the offer was serious or a kind of ploy.

On the domestic front, Sadat stepped into the shoes of a leader who ruled partly through personal charisma and partly through intimidation. Sadat changed the mix. He supervised the symbolic burning of thousands of wiretap recordings and secret police files in the courtyard of the Interior Ministry, yet the practices of wiretapping and keeping secret files continued. He jailed political opponents on more than one occasion, but he released far more to show his magnanimity. More than anything, Sadat's days as a propagandist taught him how to use images and photo opportunities to create apparent realities years before Ronald Reagan reinvented the U.S. presidency by doing the same thing. Although some considered Sadat's publicity efforts to be cynical stunts, they underestimated Sadat's sophisticated understanding of the importance of symbolism, and, further, his understanding of the role of public opinion in creating a "mood" quite apart from the exigencies of electoral politics.

In a move intended for both domestic and foreign consumption, he expelled thousands of Soviet advisers from Egypt in July 1972. In an even bolder move, Egyptian troops broke through the Bar Lev line on October 6, 1973, using water cannons to blast away a steep thirty- to sixty-foot-high sand wall on the eastern bank of the Suez Canal that had previously been thought impregnable. The dramatic crossing electrified a country demoralized by its defeat in the 1967 war. Although Egyptian troops fared less well once the element of surprise had passed and the war waged on for several weeks, even temporary success against a country that had been Egypt's foe for twenty-five years allowed Sadat to consolidate his leadership domestically.

Sadat's audacious gamble also catapulted him for the first time for consideration as a serious player in international diplomacy. Long accustomed to hanging back when his predecessor feted other world leaders, Sadat found himself being courted by Secretary of State Henry Kissinger, who had a reputation as a brilliant strategist and thinker. Sadat was being seen as a brilliant strategist in his own right, since his limited war against the Israelis resulted in the Egyptians regaining control over the Suez Canal, as well as what the Egyptian military to this day considers to be its principal victory in the modern era.

Sadat's emergence on the world stage, however, remained tied to his political success in Egypt. He understood the intimate relationship between success in the foreign affairs arena and popularity at home, which Nasser had so successfully constructed and manipulated, and he understood how gestures on the domestic scene could help his international position. He became a master at both. Sadat led Egypt away from the Soviet Union and into the waiting arms of the West. He dismantled many of the socialist features of the Egyptian state, and in so doing he impressed Western leaders with his sincerity, weakened his opponents, and enriched his friends. Just as the revolution's land reform program had attacked the power bases of the "feudal" class, Sadat's "economic opening," or *infitah,* in 1974 attacked the power base of the government oligarchy. Sadat also began a controlled opening of the political process, although never so much as to threaten his hand on power. Whereas each of these moves might be seen as expressions of a pro-Western stance, they all had important repercussions on the Egyptian domestic stage.

It was Sadat's mastery of the Egyptian stage that allowed him to be so successful on the international stage when the opportunity presented itself. From his experience in Egyptian politics, Sadat understood the importance of forming long-term and durable alliances to pursue long-term goals. His two primary goals upon coming to power were to regain the Sinai for Egypt and to improve the lackluster Egyptian economy. Although he was a nationalist, he understood that his goals could be achieved most readily with the support of an outside power.

Surveying the world in the early 1970s, Sadat decided an alliance with the United States offered the best prospects. The Soviet Union had been tested and found wanting, and Sadat saw in America's close relationship with Israel an opportunity to form his own close relationship with the United States. To this end, Sadat developed an unusual rapport with the American ambassador in Cairo, Hermann Eilts, and he assiduously cultivated friendships with each of the four U.S. presidents with whom he dealt: Nixon, Ford, Carter and Reagan. In the words of Henry Kissinger:

> He treated Nixon as a great statesman, Ford as the living manifestation of good-will, Carter as a missionary almost too decent for this world, and Reagan as the benevolent leader of a popular revolution, subtly appealing to each man's conception of himself and gaining the confidence of each.[5]

---

5   Henry Kissinger, *Years of Upheaval* (Boston: Little, Brown, 1982), p. 649.

Sadat approached each of these men with the disarming (and, at least at the beginning, counterintuitive) premise that the United States and Egypt shared deep common interests. He offered rosy visions of a common future, and he laid out a road map to get there. At several times during American-mediated peace negotiations with Israel, Sadat slipped a secret copy of his "fall-back" positions to the U.S. president, at once showing his reasonableness and enlisting American partnership in achieving his goals.

Sadat also applied his mastery of symbolism to international relations. His decision to go to Jerusalem was breathtaking in its effect, and his landing on Israeli soil irrevocably changed the nature of the Arab–Israeli conflict. In one gesture granting the Israelis the recognition they had been demanding for decades, Sadat at the same time won an American commitment to aid Egypt in recovering the lands Egypt had lost in war.

Sadat's decision to go to Jerusalem was surely the most dramatic of his life. It was dramatic not only because it utterly transformed the Middle East, but also because it was a supreme act of faith. Sadat decided to play his primary card—recognition of Israel—out of a conviction that the United States, and particularly President Carter, would not allow his effort to be in vain. The gesture becomes even more impressive when one considers that Sadat had been disappointed with Carter's election only a year before his trip to Jerusalem, and that the great trust the men had in each other had developed after only a single set of meetings between them.

Sadat's calculus depended on his assessment that he had a limited window of opportunity, and that window was closing. Without clear U.S. leadership and something approaching bilateral negotiations with the

Israelis, Egyptian claims to Sinai would surely be lost in fruitless multilateral peace negotiations in Geneva. The entropy unleashed by Sadat's dramatic breeching of the Bar Lev line would dissipate, and the sole consequence of the 1973 war would be Egyptian sovereignty over the Suez Canal. The bulk of Sinai would remain under Israeli control, and any further efforts to regain Sinai for Egypt would require a massive military confrontation with the Israelis. In that event, a larger victory would prove much harder to achieve than the tactical victory of October 6, 1973. Further, the United States was anxious for a deal in 1977, and Sadat understood the prospect of harnessing American enthusiasm for significant economic development assistance.

Sadat chose the riskiest of the options before him in November 1977, at a time when the magnitude of the rewards for his actions could not have been foreseen. Sadat gambled because he must have understood that the costs of inaction were almost as great as the costs of losing, while the possible rewards for action were much greater. Sadat, and Egypt, won much from his gamble.

Sadat's leadership style has been dismissed by some as an expression of *fahlawa*, an Egyptian peasant's shrewd combination of dissimulation and flattery in the face of power.[6] Such assessments underestimate Sadat on several levels. First, they give insufficient credit to Sadat's ability to identify and achieve his goals. Sadat was opportunistic to be sure, but he also had a keen

---

[6] For example, Raymond A. Hinnebusch, Jr., *Egyptian Politics under Sadat: The post-populist development of an authoritarian-modernizing state* (Cambridge: Cambridge University Press, 1985), pp. 80–81, and Hirst and Beeson, pp. 354–356.

sense of the "big picture" and constantly took incremental steps to bring him closer to his objectives. Second, such assessments do not account for Sadat's ability to take dramatic and forceful steps when conditions were propitious. Once he was in power, Sadat did not play cautiously on the margins but moved daringly in pursuit of his goals. Third, such assessments play into the very image Sadat created for himself—the *ibn al-balad*[7] from Mit Abul Kum who made good in the big city. The image of a village naïf helping his country may have been useful politically, but it surely does not account for the astounding success of an agitator and survivor with a truly life-long involvement in politics. It does not take *fahlawa* to explain the wisdom of not confronting those with overwhelming strength, and it certainly takes more than that to explain Sadat's mastery of the political scene once he became ascendant.

Sadat's calculations in positioning Egypt on the world stage are the subject of the presentations that follow, a product of a special conference commenced on the twentieth anniversary of Sadat's journey to Jerusalem. As they demonstrate, his actions were a combination of the personal and the political, a product of Sadat as an individual and Sadat as the president of Egypt.

Although he will always be remembered for his courageous leap toward peace, Sadat's ultimate legacy remains uncertain. The negotiations he started did not result in the end of the Arab–Israeli conflict, nor did they create a prosperous Egypt. In his last years, Sadat appears to have lost his "touch" in Egyptian politics, and in his final months he seemed to be turning oppressive.

---

[7]   Literally, "son of the land."

But it is worth remembering that Sadat's political skill brought enormous benefit to his country. Egypt now has peace on its eastern border, and in fact it faces no serious military threats from any direction. Egypt has received tens of billions of dollars of U.S. aid over the last two decades, which it has used to modernize its army and thoroughly improve its national infrastructure. Even small Egyptian villages are now connected to the electric grid, and in Egypt, the credit for that is seen to lie with Sadat rather than the United States. Egypt also has emerged as the leading state in the Arab world and in the region. Faced with a crumbling and inward-looking economy oriented toward the Soviet Union, Sadat laid the groundwork for Egyptian prosperity, even if it has not yet arrived. Sadat truly led his country, and it was his tragedy that, perhaps, he got too far ahead of the people he was leading.

The presentations that follow illustrate both the direction in which he led and the legacy of his leadership. They begin with an appreciation of the human side of Anwar Sadat by his daughter Camelia. She discusses his combination of deep nationalism and humanity, and the strength he gave to those around him by his example. Ambassador Ahmed Maher el-Sayed of Egypt, who worked on the Egyptian negotiating team during the Sadat era, lays out his perspective on the Sadat vision and its future.

The second section of this volume offers eyewitness testimony to the drama unfolding in Cairo, Jerusalem, and Washington in November 1977 as Sadat's offer to go to Jerusalem, "to the ends of the earth," became a reality. Ambassador Hermann Eilts represented the United States in Cairo, while Ambassador Eliahu Ben Elissar served as a close aide to Israeli prime minister

Menachem Begin. Kenneth Stein interviewed the principal U.S. participants in Middle East policy at the time and offers the view from Washington. The third section explores the military changes brought about by Sadat's trip to Jerusalem. Maj. Gen. (ret.) Ahmed Fakhr presents the view from within the Egyptian armed forces, and Ambassador Wat Cluverius describes the view from his position as director general of the Multinational Force and Observers that monitors the peace in Sinai. Military analyst Kenneth Pollack offers his own assessment of Sadat's role in history as a great strategist.

The fourth section examines Sadat's domestic political legacy, with analyses from three professors with intimate knowledge of Egypt and the Egyptian political system—Shimon Shamir, Saad Eddin Ibrahim, and Shibley Telhami—and the fifth concentrates on the Egyptian–Israeli relationship. In that section, Abdel Monem Said and Ehud Ya'ari detail the fruits and occassional frustrations of peace, and Ambassador Samuel Lewis offers his insights as a long-time U.S. ambassador to Israel and a veteran of Arab–Israeli peace negotiations. In the sixth section, Peter Rodman, Ambassador Robert Pelletreau, and Robert Satloff examine the Egyptian–U.S. relationship that Sadat was so important in nurturing. Finally, Assistant Secretary of State Martin Indyk assesses the fundamental importance of the peace process that Anwar Sadat began and looks ahead to the future.

The conference on which this volume is based took place in November 1997. Several major policy issues were very much on the minds of the attendees at the time, as is evidenced by the discussions following the formal presentations. Just prior to the conference, the government of Egypt announced that it would not attend the fourth Middle East and North Africa (MENA) Economic Conference in Doha, Qatar. The MENA meetings have been an integral part of the ongoing Arab–Israeli peace process, and many in Washington took the Egyptian decision not to attend the Doha Conference as an intentional snub of the United States. Also in November, a crisis was brewing between Iraqi dictator Saddam Hussein and the UN Special Commission established to investigate and dismantle his program to develop and deploy weapons of mass destructions. The resolution of that confrontation was unclear in November; even now, with a UN-brokered diplomatic resolution averting war, the final outcome remains cloudy.

The searching discussions that followed the panels are a sign of just how relevant Sadat's diplomacy remains today, twenty years after his historic trip to Jerusalem.

one

Anwar Sadat and His Vision

Camelia Anwar Sadat
Ahmed Maher el-Sayed

Camelia Anwar Sadat recalls that her father not only was a family man, nationalist, and leader, but he also represented a "school" to those who faced challenges in their lives. Amb. Ahmed Maher el-Sayed, Egypt's envoy to the United States, describes Sadat's vision and its future.

Camelia Anwar Sadat

President Anwar Sadat was more than a father to me and a president to a nation. He represented a school. The lessons of the "Sadat school" extended far beyond book learning. President Sadat set an example for personal conduct, self-respect, and the power of education that has been an inspiration to me my entire life.

President Sadat's personality was formed in the small village where he grew up, Mit Abul Kum. He was one of thirteen children born to an Army clerk posted in the Sudan. His grandmother raised him mostly, and she left him with two legacies. The first was a belief in the importance of sincerity. Word of lying gets around quickly in a small village, and his grandmother brought him up to be a person of honor who kept his word.

My great-grandmother's other legacy was to raise my father to be an Egyptian patriot. President Sadat was born during the British occupation of Egypt, and from his infancy he heard stories about the injustices inflicted on the Egyptian people. One such story involved a conflict in the neighboring village between British troops and some local youths, during which a British soldier had died. The British responded by sentencing the Egyptians to death without so much as an investigation. Most of the youths quietly walked to the hastily erected scaffolds, but one, named Zahran, walked with his head held high. As he went to his death he proclaimed, "I am dying to free Egypt." Throughout his life, my father saw himself as Zahran, as a true patriot.

My great-grandmother also told my father stories about Mahatma Gandhi, who was then coming to prominence as a leader for Indian independence. When he was seven or eight, my father was so taken with the image of being a Gandhi to his people that he got a walking stick and took off most of his clothes and marched around the village. He got pneumonia. His family put him to bed and said, "Forget about freeing your country right now. You're still too young." Still, the idea was in his head from an early age.

He went to a *kuttab*, a religious school, for his early education. He went on to high school and attended the military academy in one of the first classes opened up to students who were not from prominent families. Soon after graduation the British jailed him for activities against the occupation. He was in and out of jail for the next eight years.

Anwar Sadat was part of the group that made the revolution in 1952, and he remained active in politics in subsequent years. He became the speaker of the People's Assembly and then vice president of the Republic. When President Gamal Abdel Nasser died in 1970, my father became president.

Anwar Sadat did not campaign for the government positions he held, including that of the presidency. An inner strength and an inner light always guided him; others recognized his strengths and appointed him on that basis. When I was having problems in my own life, he said to me, "Problems don't make you. When you walk with your head held high, you will gain self-esteem. You will be able to see problems as the small matters that they are. If details do not deserve attention, do not give them attention." He also urged me to pull back from matters in order to see them more clearly. "Envision things and calculate them," he urged me; "understand a goal and then plan how to reach it."

He envisioned and planned, but he did not overwhelm people with his insights and strength. He preferred to keep his views to himself. He never showed his power. This was a response to his environment growing up, an environment in which showing power often invited confrontation.

President Sadat was a great believer in self-education. He read widely in political science, history, anthropology, strategy, and a host of other fields. He believed that knowledge from one field enhanced understanding of another. He also knew personally how knowledge could make a difference. At one point in 1958, before a trip to Iran, he learned a Persian proverb. Relations between Egypt and Iran at the time were somewhat strained. At the end of his speech, he recited this Persian proverb. The Shah was very impressed, and he and my father formed a long and close friendship. It was all because of this little bit of knowledge.

It was this intellectual curiosity that led President Sadat to begin to envision an end to the Arab–Israeli conflict. He used his understanding and insight to show us all that there are mothers and sisters and cousins on both sides of this conflict, and all are bereaved when war breaks out. His courageous trip to Jerusalem began to dismantle all of the hatred and suspicion that thirty years of war had created. He understood that we are all the children of Abraham, and he taught us all to see this truth.

President Sadat was not a man who was afraid of risks. He risked everything he had for his trip to Jerusalem. Had it failed, he would have lost everything. But he did not fail, and the result of his courage is the peace that we enjoy today. His courage foreshadowed the courage other world leaders have shown in later

years: Ronald Reagan signing the Strategic Arms
Limitations Treaty with the Soviet Union despite
previously calling the USSR "The Evil Empire," Mikhail
Gorbachev introducing *glasnost* and *perestroika* to a
country that desperately needed both. The Berlin Wall
fell in 1989. Why? Because of the principles that my
father lived by: coexistence, good neighborliness, and
peace between extended branches of the same family.
Nelson Mandela is another credit to the "Sadat school,"
for he led South Africa's peaceful transition to
democracy after so many years of white rule.

I am very proud to be a product of the Sadat school,
and I appreciate the opportunity to pay a tribute to the
professor of that school, my father, Anwar Sadat.

Ahmed Maher el-Sayed

Twenty years ago, in a bold and visionary move, Anwar Sadat landed in Jerusalem. It was a giant step into uncharted territory by a man who had overcome prejudices and pain to open the way to a reconciliation—a move that, a few days before, had not even crossed the wildest imaginations. Although people still entertain doubts about the utility and practical impact of landing the first man on the moon, nobody doubts the impact of Sadat's landing. Despite difficulties and obstacles, it continued for a long time to be a star of hope over the land of peace that had for years been torn by wars and strife.

Sadat's journey was made possible because, on the other side of the divide, another man of vision was also at the helm. Prime Minister Menachem Begin was courageously able to overcome many of his ideological warts and illusions, which he shared for some time with many other Israelis. After arduous and sometimes painful negotiations, Egypt and Israel reached an agreement that put an end to the bilateral aspect of their dispute and established the basis to settle the Arab–Israeli conflict and provide for the historic reconciliation between the sons of Abraham.

Unfortunately, myths die slowly, and illusions refuse to give way to realities. On the Israeli side, some saw the Egyptian–Israeli peace not as a precursor but as a substitute for a comprehensive settlement. They saw in Camp David a sort of *carte blanche* to continue to negate the existence and the rights of the Palestinian people and to maintain their occupation of Arab territories. On the Arab side, many continued to entertain

the impossible dream of restoring their territories
without negotiations and without recognizing Israel and
coexisting with it in peace and security.

Those myths and illusions—on both sides—could
not alter the essence of what Sadat had achieved, and
reality finally caught up with them. Years later, because
men of vision on both sides accepted their responsibilities, the world was able to watch old and fierce enemies
sign a Palestinian–Israeli peace agreement on the South
Lawn of the White House. Months later, the world
watched again as Jordan and Israel signed a peace treaty
in the desert. Progress was achieved on the Syrian–
Israeli and Lebanese–Israeli tracks.

None of this was easy, but it was possible because of
the courage and determination of the participants. It was
possible as well because Egypt had established the basis
for peace: land for peace, confidence-building measures,
and security guarantees on both sides. Within this
framework, the parties had a sense of direction that
helped them through difficult times. The parties were
like travelers on the same train. They could disagree,
quarrel, and bicker, but the direction of the train was
predetermined.

Suddenly, one of the parties decided to leave the
train and take the opposite direction. Since then, the
peace process—despite the efforts of the United States,
Egypt, and all people of goodwill—has slipped into a
coma. The hopes that had begun to materialize vanished
because a lack of historical vision, the mistaken reading
of realities, and an attitude of contempt for the other had
taken over. Dreams were shattered and security was
endangered, encouraging forces of extremism on both
sides to grow and create havoc.

The peace process is not dead, but it may be terminally ill unless the participants do something to maintain Sadat's legacy. This is the responsibility of all the peoples of the region. This is what the United States is trying to do, and I am sure is determined to continue to do, as the essential and indispensable friend of peace. This is what President Husni Mubarak is exerting every effort to achieve, using all the tools of diplomacy at his disposal. He is using his wide contacts and the confidence he enjoys as a statesman with vision and courage, as a leader who believes in and practices plain talk. He communicates with clarity and objectivity how he sees matters from his vantage point. He is inspired by a deep desire to see the comprehensive peace that has been Egypt's aim since Sadat's initiative, and which will ensure peace, security, and development for all the peoples of the region on the basis of equality and reconciliation, in the context of international legitimacy.

Nobody should have to pay again the terrible price of war—not in Israel, not in Palestine, not in Lebanon, not anywhere. This reminds me of a sentence I read yesterday in the Israeli newspaper *Ha'aretz*: "If Israel continues to wallow in obsolete territorial conceptions from twenty years and several wars ago, it will continue to pay the familiar price in blood." And, I may add, not only will Israel, but all the peoples of the area will do so. What these people want is the right to pursue happiness, to recall the phrasing of the U.S. Declaration of Independence. They want dignity and prosperity, in peace and security. Sadat's initiative is not only a textbook matter; it is a living legacy. It is not the past; it is the future striving to blossom.

The scholars, leaders, and journalists here today should work to ensure that confidence be restored. This will be achieved not on the basis of a fixation on one matter, but on the sincere implementation of all agreements. This will be achieved by assuming responsibilities instead of trying to find pretexts to evade them, by clearly defining security for both parties.

What is needed to achieve it? Treating symptoms and causes at the same time and with the same vigor; recognizing that the right of self-determination and other rights of peoples are not the exclusivity of one party to the exclusion of others.

Sadat dreamed of a truly new Middle East, one in which free peoples, each living in their own sovereign states, freely cooperated with their neighbors for the common good: Palestine, Israel, Egypt, Syria, Lebanon, Jordan. This is the only viable map of the Middle East. Let us rededicate ourselves to this vision, thereby ensuring a better future for the next generation, and perhaps enjoying some of it ourselves if we work hard enough. Sadat's legacy is alive. Where is Begin's, Rabin's, and Peres's? They may all have been, at times, found wanting, but how we miss their visionary courage.

two

Sadat's Journey

Hermann Frederick Eilts
Eliahu Ben Elissar
Kenneth W. Stein

In November 1977, officials in the Egyptian, Israeli, and American governments witnessed something they had thought impossible happen before their eyes. Anwar Sadat announced on November 9 that he would go to Jerusalem to pursue peace, and the seemingly far-fetched idea became a reality less than two weeks later. In the section that follows, two eye-witnesses to those events—former U.S. Ambassador to Egypt Hermann Eilts and Menachem Begin's close aide Eliahu Ben Elissar— recall the uncertainty and drama of those days. In addition, historian Kenneth Stein assesses the reasons for Sadat's trip as viewed from Washington.

Hermann Frederick Eilts

Twenty years ago, Anwar Sadat made his historic trip to Jerusalem. In the course of twenty years, one tends to forget exactly what went into a trip of that sort, but it is worth bearing in mind—as we worry about the fact that the peace process is not going as well as one would like it to—that it took six long years after the October 1973 War before peace between Israel and Egypt occurred. Perhaps a little patience is not out of order in this situation.

In the short space I have been given, I want to discuss the road to Jerusalem—specifically, the year 1977, as it affected President Anwar Sadat. When the year started, he was not feeling good about the peace process. His good friend, President Gerald Ford, expected to be reelected in 1976. Ford promised Sadat that upon his reelection, he would abandon the interim approach to Middle East peace that he had been following up to that time and would pursue a comprehensive peace. This was something that Sadat wanted, because he had come to the conclusion that interim peace steps were no longer feasible. He felt he had been giving too much away, and if he continued the current process to its conclusion he would be left at the end not having recovered everything that he wanted.

When Jimmy Carter was elected, Sadat was initially quite upset. He felt that President Carter had been too pro-Israeli in his campaign statements. Upon reflection, however, he became less anxious about Carter. As he put it, "He's a man of religion, and any man who has so much religion must not be all bad."

Sadat was pleased that Carter also decided to pursue a comprehensive peace, and that Carter's goal was to get the parties to Geneva. Sadat was anxious to go to Geneva at the beginning of 1977, because he saw this as the only way to achieve a comprehensive peace. In the spring of 1977, the Carter administration undertook a series of steps to get the parties to Geneva, it was hoped by the end of the year. The first step in that process was a meeting with Prime Minister Yitzhak Rabin in the United States and then a meeting with Sadat. Sadat was not particularly happy when President Carter said to him, "If you want me to move toward peace, to urge the Israeli government to move toward peace, you have got to accept the fact that there must be diplomatic relations and normalization" between Egypt and Israel. Sadat had not, at that point, expected such a demand. He said, "Well, that can wait for the next generation." To his credit, Carter said, "No, that must be part of it." And so it gradually got into Sadat's thinking.

Then there was a meeting between President Carter and Syrian president Hafiz al-Asad in Geneva. Sadat was upset about that, not so much that the meeting had taken place, but that out of it came the suggestion of a joint Arab delegation to peace talks. Sadat did not like that; he wanted separate delegations. But he accepted the concept of a joint delegation, because it was the only way to allow the Palestinians to take part. Israel would not have accepted Palestinian participation at that time, but in the context of a joint delegation, this was possible.

In May 1977, Likud won the elections in Israel. This upset Sadat. He said to me, "You know, there's only one good man in that new government, and that is Moshe Dayan. And this fellow Ezer Weizman, he's a war monger. We know him." I mention that at this point, because after the trip to Jerusalem, as I will relate below, things had changed completely.

Then there was the question of working out something with the Soviets; all, remember, in the context of getting to Geneva. Some revisionists have argued that Sadat did not want that. In fact, he was not at all displeased about the arrangement with the Soviets. The United States had worked out a system under which the parties—the Arabs and the Israelis—would have direct talks. The two superpowers would not participate directly in those talks; they would be outside. It was firmly assumed that the two parties would not be able to agree, and they would come out and request the help of the superpowers. The Soviets had no relations with Israel; hence, there was little that they could provide. The United States had relations with both, and so it could have acted in a mediating capacity. Whether it would have worked out or not, no one can say.

On the road to Geneva, the typical problem that has bedeviled negotiations between Israel and the Arab states surfaced once again. The parties could not agree on what the agenda should be: what should come first, what should come second, what should come third.

Sadat became increasingly frustrated about that. President Carter finally proposed, "Let us go to Geneva without an agenda and make the determination of the agenda the first item of business." Sadat accepted that, but to his horror and distress, there was no response from the Syrians. Weeks went by, and Sadat began to say, "Peace is slipping through my fingers for procedural reasons."

Then President Carter sent a handwritten letter to President Sadat, asking him to take some dramatic step. He hoped that Sadat could influence the Syrians or the

Palestinians, but at that point Egypt's relations with Syria were not that good, nor were they good with the Palestinians.

Out of this call for a dramatic step came—and this was Sadat's own idea—the idea of a trip to Jerusalem. The initial thought of direct talks had come from several sources. Various of Sadat's Jewish friends in Vienna, Paris, and London had urged him to have direct talks with the Israelis, as had the King of Morocco. But Sadat was a dramatist, first and foremost, and the idea of going to Jerusalem would incorporate direct talks and offer the possibility of presenting the Arab point of view in the Knesset. Further, coming on the Eid, on the Muslim holiday, it would have great dramatic effect in the Arab world.

Sadat made a speech to the Egyptian People's Assembly on November 9. He was not sure whether he was going to say that he was going to the Knesset. It was not in the original text of the speech. Sadat used to make long speeches, and he would put aside his text from time to time and extemporize. He was about four-fifths through with what was a two-hour speech. The cabinet was seated out front, and Yasir Arafat was there. Next to me, in the diplomatic box, was Abu Iyad. Close to the end, Sadat put his speech aside and spoke about going to the Knesset. It was interesting. Everybody cheered. Everybody applauded, even Yasir Arafat. Abu Iyad did not look particularly happy about it, but nevertheless it had been done.

The next day an American congressional delegation visited Sadat. As one might imagine, they were deeply interested in the announcement. They asked, "Are you going to go to Jerusalem? Do you mean it?" He said, "Yes, I mean it." Congressman Henry Waxman of

California said, "Mr. President, I don't believe that
you're going to go to Jerusalem." Sadat replied, "Why
don't you come with me?"

A second congressional delegation arrived, and they
were equally interested. Sadat said, "I will go if I get an
invitation." I told Sadat he could expect an invitation
from Prime Minister Begin. He said, "That's fine. If I
get one, fine; if I don't, fine. But just one thing: I cannot
accept the invitation directly. It must come through
President Carter."

And so, when Prime Minister Begin sent his
invitation, there was a brief covering message from
President Carter transmitting the invitation. It was on
Wednesday, November 16 and he was leaving for
Damascus at 10 a.m. I got it in a flash telegram at about
5 a.m., and I did not want Sadat to leave for Damascus
until he had the message.

I got Sadat out of bed where he was staying, at the
Barrages. He was sort of grumpy; he did not like to be
awakened that early. I read the invitation to him. He
said, "Read it again." And I read it. And he said, "You
know, this is a nice invitation."

At that point, Vice President Husni Mubarak came
in, and Sadat said, "Read this to Husni." I read it to the
vice president, who had no comment on it. But then
Mubarak said, "Mr. President, whatever you decide to
do, you'd better not say anything until you come back
from Damascus, because if something is said about this
before you go to Damascus, you may not come back."
Sadat said, "That's fine," and they set off for Damascus.
I went along to the airport and said to Vice President
Mubarak, "Now, when is he planning to go?" Mubarak
said, "On Saturday"—in three days' time. I said, "Well,

the Israelis had better be told about this." "Oh," he said, "nobody can tell them; nobody. No, no. Can't do that." I said, "Somebody has to tell them." Mubarak said, "Sadat wants to send the advance team on Friday," and I said, "That makes it even more important that we tell the Israelis." Mubarak said, "But he hasn't given you an answer." I said, "You have, Mr. Vice President."

Finally, Mubarak said, "All right. You send a message to the Israeli government," through the U.S. ambassador, Samuel Lewis, saying, "If a certain president wants to visit Israel on a Saturday, what should be the earliest time that he should arrive?" A message came back through Ambassador Lewis that said, "If a certain president wants to visit Israel on a Saturday, he should come anytime after 6 o'clock in the evening."

At this point, Sadat had still not given me an answer. He said, "Meet me in Ismailia tomorrow, when I get back from Damascus, and I'll give you the answer." So the vice president and I went to Ismailia the following day. A small group of people were there: the vice president, the prime minister, the minister of defense, and some of the presidential secretariat.

Sadat arrived about 3 o'clock. He was exhausted. It had been a very difficult session in Damascus. He said, "What have you got for me?" I said, "Mr. President, what have you got for me? The invitation from Mr. Begin." "Oh, yes," he said, "I will go on Saturday."

At that point, somebody rushed in to the garden where we were sitting and said, "The photographers are outside with the TV people. They know something is up. They don't know what it is, but they are there." Sadat said, "That's fine. Bring them in, in a minute."

He said to me, "Where is that invitation?" I said, "Mr. President, I gave it to you yesterday." He said,

"What did I do with it?" I said, "You gave it to the vice president." He said, "Husni, what have you done with the invitation? Where is it?" Husni said, "I left it in Cairo."

The photographers were waiting. Fortunately, it was on the eve of the Eid, and I had a single-page Eid greeting from the American president, which is always sent to Muslim leaders. Sadat said, "That will do."

Sadat seated himself near the wall, puffed his pipe, and the photographers were allowed in. As one can imagine, they came in like a storming herd of buffalo. Sadat greeted them, and he said, "Now, Hermann, what have you got here?" I said, "Mr. President, an invitation from Prime Minister Begin." He opened it so nobody could get behind him to see what it was that he was reading. He puffed his pipe, nodded his head, and said, "Please tell Mr. Begin, through President Carter, that I accept."

The photographers left, all believing that they had seen the original invitation, which, as it turned out, was still in Cairo. But no damage was done. Then he said, "I have one other bit of business." I excused myself, but Sadat said "No, you stay."

Egypt's foreign minister and deputy prime minister, Ismail Fahmy, had objected to the visit to Jerusalem and had sent his resignation. Sadat ordered the vice president, "Get back to Cairo and accept Fahmy's resignation." Much to his credit, Prime Minister Mamduh Salem, who did not care for Fahmy, said, "Let me talk to Ismail." "No," said the president, "he's done it too often. He goes. When you get back, name Muhammad Riad," Fahmy's assistant, "as the new foreign minister."

We all got back on the helicopter and returned to
Cairo. As one can imagine, I was anxious to get word
out. I was seated next to General Abdel Ghani al-
Gamassy. He had a long face; he was very unhappy
about this. Fahmy had told me previously, "If the
president does something I don't like, not only will I
resign, but so will Gamassy." I told Gamassy, "General,
I hope you're going to stick with the president." He
responded, "I don't think the president is doing the right
thing, but I'm a soldier, and I will stay with the
president."

We got back to Cairo, and I was sending off
messages when suddenly I heard on the radio that
Muhammad Riad had resigned as foreign minister. I
called him. I said, "Muhammad, you've just been
named." He said, "Well, the vice president called me,
and he said, 'You're to be the foreign minister.'"
Muhammad Riad asked, "Could I think about this a bit?"
And he said, "The next thing I heard was that I had
resigned, when I had never even accepted the position."

The next day Ambassador Lewis briefed the Israeli
prime minister and I briefed Sadat. And off Sadat went.
The night Sadat left for Israel, I was with a group of
Egyptians. Some were furious that he was doing this.
Others were greatly cheered; peace might finally be here.
There was a third body that was convinced that Sadat,
upon his arrival in Israel, would be assassinated. For
some, that was a very real worry, but it never worried
Sadat. He was a fatalist about these things.

In any case, Sadat went, came back a few days later,
and said, "This has been a great visit." Yet, Dayan was
no longer the favorite. Why? Because Dayan had ridden
from the airport to Jerusalem in a car with Boutros
Boutros-Ghali, and Dayan had pressed Boutros that

Egypt should sign a separate peace, and Sadat did not like this one bit.

Now the hero was Defense Minister Ezer Weizman. Everything was about Ezer. Wonderful man. He had had some leg ailment, but he had saluted Sadat with his cane, and Sadat liked that. Sadat's brother had been killed in a war with Israel, and Weizman had lost his son. Now Weizman was it. That was probably one of the luckiest breaks, because in the ensuing months, on the military side, Weizman and Gamassy got along famously. At one point, Gamassy even said to me, "If these politicians would only get out of the business and allow Ezer and myself to handle it, we could have peace in eight hours." They obviously could not do that, but I mention this simply as an indication of the sense of confidence that had developed very quickly among the professional military people.

It is also worth remembering that three months after the trip to Jerusalem, which Sadat saw as breaking through the psychological barrier, he was completely down and out. He felt that there had not been an adequate response from the Israeli side. Prime Minister Begin had gone to Egypt, they met in Ismailia on December 25, and the prime minister had presented some ideas.

Many in the Israeli delegation felt that Sadat would have accepted these ideas had it not been for some of his advisers. The fact of the matter is that Sadat did not like them at all. Sadat was never a man for detail, and when he did not like something, all too often, instead of specifically saying so, he would simply grunt, "Hmm. Hmm, hmm." The Israelis misinterpreted his grunts.

By the middle of January, Sadat was so down and out that he was talking about resigning. He felt his policy had been a failure. Mubarak was very upset about this. I was very upset about it. Jihan Sadat, the president's wife, was very upset about it. He remained in office and the peace process continued, in large part because the United States first arranged the Leeds Castle conference, and then, subsequently, the Camp David conference.

I mention this because it is worth reminding ourselves that Sadat, despite his enormous courage, found the road to Jerusalem an extraordinarily difficult one.

Eliahu Ben Elissar

It all started in Jerusalem with Menachem Begin's arrival to power. Long before May 1977, when Likud won control of the Knesset and Begin became prime minister, he thought that the policy of the State of Israel should be oriented toward Egypt and not, as it used to be, toward Jordan.

Begin always had the idea that the first Arab country that would be able and perhaps willing to reach a peace settlement with Israel would be Egypt. This fact is generally poorly known, both in Israel and abroad. I am sure of this fact. I heard it from Begin himself, probably in 1974 or 1975. I know that this was his approach and his idea.

Within six weeks of assuming the post of prime minister, Begin told the director of the Mossad, Yitzhak Hoffi, to meet secretly with an envoy sent by President Anwar Sadat. Then, on September 16, 1977, Egyptian deputy prime minister Hassan al-Tuhami met with none other than Israeli foreign minister Moshe Dayan in Morocco. This was two months before Sadat's historic voyage to Jerusalem.

Interestingly enough, King Hassan II of Morocco, who was instrumental in arranging this meeting, did not believe that Egypt was ready to achieve a settlement with Israel. He thought that the first Arab country that Israel should approach should be Syria. Dayan rejected this proposal right away. He told the king that Hafiz al-Asad would probably be the last to sign a peace settlement with Israel.

The road to Jerusalem began with President Sadat's speech to the Parliament in Cairo on Wednesday,

November 9, 1977. In Jerusalem the news came the same afternoon, and Israelis treated it as we did many other speeches delivered by Arab leaders. Nobody believed it.

Nobody believed it, but the next day the *Jerusalem Post* quoted an anonymous "top aide of Prime Minister Begin" saying that if President Sadat wished to come to Israel, he "would be more than welcome here" and "accorded a proper reception."[1] On Thursday, November 10, Prime Minister Begin released, in his own name, a communiqué to Kol Yisrael (Israeli radio) welcoming a visit from President Sadat.

Saturday night, Begin spoke at a political event in Tel Aviv and reporters asked him, "What about Sadat's declaration? Is it serious; is it not serious?" For the first time, Begin invited Sadat to come to Israel. He said, "If President Sadat really means it, then *Ahlan wa-Sahlan.*"[2]

On Monday night, President Sadat said that he was ready to come to Israel and speak to the Knesset in Jerusalem. Begin said, "I am very happy. This is good news." Those of us in the Foreign Ministry still did not believe that this was going to happen, although we did begin very preliminary preparations.

That same Monday, U.S. Ambassador to Israel Samuel Lewis came to see Prime Minister Begin, and said to him, "President Sadat wants an invitation." Begin said, "In the name of the State of Israel and the government of Israel, I invite President Sadat to come to Israel."

The next day, Lewis came back to the prime minister and said, "I am sorry, Mr. Prime Minister, President

---

[1]   Anan Safadi, "Sadat 'ready to come to Knesset' to talk peace," *Jerusalem Post*, November 10, 1977, p. 1.
[2]   "Welcome," in Arabic.

Sadat does not suffice himself with an oral invitation; he wants a written invitation." It was only when Lewis said Sadat needed a written invitation that we started believing that this visit was really going to happen. Begin wrote the letter; it was the first time that the prime minister of Israel wrote an official letter to the president of the Arab Republic of Egypt, with all the regalia, signing "Prime Minister of Israel." We still did not know that the visit would occur that weekend.

How was the Israeli government to prepare? It is like trying to go to the moon. Israel was ready to welcome President Sadat as the president of a friendly country, although Israel and Egypt were still in a state of war. At the very least, the Israeli military orchestra needed to learn to play the Egyptian national anthem. Where could it get the sheet music? I called up Ambassador Lewis and said, "Please ask your ambassador in Cairo immediately to send us the Egyptian national anthem." I told the orchestra, "Take it from the Cairo radio. You don't need the sheet music. Just start practicing."

The government started working on preparations for the visit. One can imagine the preparation required for something of this kind. Journalists started streaming to Israel, and by Saturday there were 2,500 foreign correspondents in the country. This was something which was unheard of.

When a sign came from the tower that Sadat's plane had entered Israeli air space, and even when the plane landed, it still seemed unreal.

When President Sadat and Prime Minister Begin arrived at the King David Hotel in Jerusalem, they went up to President Sadat's suite. This was the very first meeting between Sadat and Begin. It was the most important meeting to take place during the whole

process, until the ultimate signature of the peace treaty.
Begin suggested to Sadat that whatever happens between
them, they solve the problems between Egypt and Israel
by peaceful means. Sadat said, "Yes, this is what we will
do." They emerged from their meeting, and Begin
declared several times, "No more war. No more
bloodshed." Sadat kept declaring, "No more war, since
the October War. No more war." This was the basic
agreement.

The remainder of the process took time and caused
frustration, disappointments, and crises. In this regard,
the diplomats proved slower-moving than the soldiers, as
if the latter better knew the price of war. I will never
forget what General Abdel Ghani al-Gamassy told me at
the Ismailia meeting of December 25, 1977. He turned to
me and said of the diplomats, "They are dragging behind
us." In spite of all the frustrations, however, the Begin
administration had a feeling that, yes, President Sadat
intended to reach a peaceful accommodation with Israel.

Israel did not believe at that stage that President
Sadat would be ready to sign a full-fledged peace treaty.
There was good evidence for this assessment. On
Sunday, November 20, Moshe Dayan asked President
Sadat, "When you talk peace, do you have in mind a
peace treaty with Israel?" And President Sadat answered,
"No, absolutely not, not a peace treaty. This will be a
peace according to the United Nations Charter." Still, we
in government believed in the understanding that Begin
and Sadat were able to reach: that there would be no
bloodshed, that there would be no war and no violence,
whatever happens.

I would like to make two points on the process itself.
Many observers believe that when Dayan and Tuhami
met in Morocco, Dayan actually promised Tuhami that

the whole of Sinai would be returned by Israel to Egypt. I was very close to that meeting, and I do not believe that Dayan ever made such a promise to Tuhami. I am not saying that territorial matters were not raised; of course they were. I am not saying that Tuhami did not state, very precisely, the Egyptian view; of course he had. But Tuhami did not get a commitment from Israel for the return of the totality of Sinai to Egypt.

The second point regards Camp David. Neither leader emerged from Camp David the way he went into it. I am convinced that Sadat did not believe that he would have to sign a peace treaty with Israel. I am sure that Begin did not think that Israel would have to relinquish the control over the totality of Sinai. Looking back today, it seems as if both leaders had very precise goals in their minds, and as it always happens in this kind of circumstance, neither got 100 percent of what he desired.

Yes, Sadat wanted the whole Sinai returned to Egypt, and he wanted to solve the Palestinian issue, and he probably wanted all of what he considered to be Arab territories to be returned to the Arab countries. Begin envisioned saving the Land of Israel for Israel. This meant, for him, that there would be only one sovereignty, Israeli sovereignty, existing between the Mediterranean and the Jordan River. Autonomy would be granted to the Palestinian Arabs who lived in this territory—not sovereignty, but autonomy. Such autonomy would not be territorial, because territorial autonomy is oriented toward sovereignty. It would be personal autonomy.

Each leader got what was most important for him. One got Sinai, and the other got the exercise of a single sovereignty, Israeli sovereignty, over the territory between the Mediterranean and Jordan. The rest was very important, as well, and they simply did not get it.

It was very important for Begin to have the El-Arish/Sharm al-Shaykh line for Israel. It was very important to have the Sinai air force bases for Israel. It was of the utmost importance for Begin to have the settlements created by the Labor government in Sinai for Israel. He had never thought of relinquishing the settlements to Egypt, but he could not keep those settlements if he wanted to achieve his primary goal. Sadat's fate was similar. He could not achieve everything. Peace was important, and Sinai was important. The Palestinian issue was important, too, but he could not get all that he wanted.

Begin wanted a peace treaty right away; he had to pay for it. Sadat did not want a peace treaty; he had to pay for it, as well. But both men wanted peace. Sadat did not trust Begin in the beginning. He learned to trust him. Begin did not trust Sadat in the beginning. He learned to trust him.

From even before he came to power, Begin's orientation was always toward peace with Egypt. This is why both leaders, who came to this process with clean hands and clean intentions, could meet so quickly. Ultimately they were able to achieve this wonderful situation of a full-fledged peace treaty between the two nations, and thus introduce a revolutionarily historic situation into the Middle East.

Kenneth W. Stein

Anwar Sadat's trip to Jerusalem in November 1977 represented the remarkable confluence of a fertile environment for diplomatic progress and a leader who saw how he could use that environment to achieve his goals. I will discuss below three characteristics of the negotiating environment, and three decisions Sadat made to capitalize on that environment.

The first characteristic was that the Arab countries wanted Israel to return the land it had taken in the 1967 war. Since 1967, all Arab–Israeli peace negotiations have centered on the fundamental issue of land for peace. It was clear to Sadat and to a few other Arab leaders in the early 1970s that for Egypt to regain the entire Sinai peninsula, it would have to do so in the context of a negotiated settlement with the Israelis.

The second characteristic was a high degree of American interest and involvement in a peace process. The United States interjected itself, interceded— intruded, one might say—into the Israeli–Egyptian disengagement negotiations right after the October 1973 War and has played a dominant role in Arab–Israeli diplomacy ever since. Leadership in this endeavor came straight from the White House: first from President Richard Nixon through Secretary of State Henry Kissinger and, later on, from President Jimmy Carter, at least through the end of 1977.

Beginning in the mid-1970s, the United States took a paternalistic interest in this negotiating process. Washington considered it "our baby." America sought to "shoe-horn" the Soviet Union out of the Middle East, and it did so successfully. It did so hesitantly, it did so haltingly, it did so repeatedly, and it did so with two disengagement agreements, but it happened. The Sinai II agreement in September 1975 was probably the most important, because it physically placed 200 Americans in the middle of Sinai. That, more than anything else, assured that if the Egyptians and the Israelis wanted to go to war, they were going to have to do it over American bodies. U.S. presence was a physical restraint against going to war.

Toward the end of Gerald Ford's administration, the United States began talking about a more comprehensive peace. Deputy Assistant Secretary of State Harold Saunders appeared before the House Foreign Affairs Committee in November 1975 and made comments about how the Palestinians had to be part of the negotiating process. The Brookings Institution issued a report in December 1975, entitled "Toward Peace in the Middle East," that discussed the timeliness of a comprehensive settlement. Zbigniew Brzezinski and Cyrus Vance participated in the preparation of that report, and they later became part of the Carter foreign policy team. After the 1975 disengagement agreement, even Henry Kissinger spoke about Palestinian political autonomy in his testimony before the Senate. Thus, the process leading toward a peace settlement was relatively well-defined well before the personalities that one speaks about with such lovingness and candor entered into the scene and became the primary participants.

U.S. policymakers' increasing engagement in an Arab–Israeli peace settlement coincided with a convergence of remarkable personalities, and this is the third important characteristic to remember. The fledgling peace process happened to have, at that particular moment in time, a rather incredible triad of individuals whose ideas, passions, personalities, styles, and characteristics permitted an interlocking—an interconnectedness—that allowed this process to proceed in 1977. This is the negotiating environment's third characteristic—the personalities.

It was extraordinary that Jimmy Carter would find himself able to accept and understand Anwar Sadat; both were farmers, men of religion. Sadat was a man of vision, a man whom Carter felt he could truly trust. In return, Sadat had an incredible reservoir of goodwill for Jimmy Carter. The relevance of the commitment that the two gentlemen had to one another cannot be understated. This is what Carter said about their relationship:

> I think that the faith that he [Sadat] put in me was to protect Egyptian interests. No matter what I did, he felt that I would never lie to him. He felt that, if I told him something that the Israelis said or the United States would do, he could depend on it. And it was not something that I had to build or orchestrate. It was kind of an immediate sharing of trust. And when somebody puts implicit faith in you, you are just not going to betray them. And I felt the same way with him.

> And so I thought, after meeting, that as far as the long-term war between Egypt and Israel was concerned, I had a card to play in my pocket, and his name was Anwar Sadat, and when the time came when I really needed some help, that I could depend upon him. Sadat was acting under the duality of the pressures that were interconnected but conflicting. He saw me as his ally; I saw him as my friend.

"And I think," Carter said, parenthetically, afterward, "Begin was jealous of it."[1]

That was probably very true: Israeli prime minister Menachem Begin was jealous of the relationship Carter had with Sadat. That jealousy came into play in the relationship that Carter developed, ultimately, with Begin, and Begin with Carter. Begin and Carter developed a working relationship; Carter came to understand Begin and Begin's commitment to the Land of Israel, but Carter's relationship with Sadat was special.

Sadat also sensed that Begin could be trusted. He sent out feelers to test Begin and his advisers to see if Israel was prepared to trade land for peace. He sent messages to Israel via Romania and via Iran, and through direct discussions in Morocco—all of those played a role in Sadat's assessment. These three men, with their respective strengths of character, intersected at a very peculiar moment, and at a very significant time. Because of it, an agreement was possible.

Carter's relationships with Sadat and Begin were not replicated throughout his administration. In particular the Israelis placed less trust in National Security Adviser Zbigniew Brzezinski and Secretary of State Cyrus Vance. In addition, the Israeli leadership was never able to establish the close relationship with Carter that Sadat had. Between Israel and the Americans, there was a crustiness in the relationship. Carter's relationship with Sadat lacked that friction and tension.

The long-term impact of the Americans' relatively closer relationship with Anwar Sadat than with his Israeli counterparts was that Sadat used Secretary of

---

[1]   Quotations for this presentation were taken from the author's longer project and completed book manuscript, which focuses on U.S. involvement in the peace process in the 1970s.

State Kissinger and later President Carter as "ambassadors" of Egypt to Israel, in a real sense of the word. Anwar Sadat was very capable of using the U.S. secretary of state, and then the U.S. president, to plead his case to Israel. In that way, Anwar Sadat forever intruded himself and Egypt into the special relationship that had existed for many years between Israel and the United States.

With this context in mind, why did Sadat go to Jerusalem? Sadat made three judgments. The first was that surprise could be a highly useful tool in international diplomacy. Sadat loved surprises; he had made surprising moves before in regional and international relations. He surprised Henry Kissinger in 1972 when he kicked the Soviets out of Cairo, with no warning and with no *quid pro quo* requested in return from the United States. He surprised the Syrians, his co-conspirators in war, the next year during the October War, when Egyptian troops suddenly stopped advancing after gaining ten kilometers east of the Suez Canal. Then, Sadat went to Jerusalem, and he surprised everyone. Yet, one has to understand his visit to Jerusalem in the context of his political predilections. As Sadat was pursuing one option, often times he was simultaneously preparing the ground to pursue another. He would talk about a comprehensive peace and going to Geneva while sending his deputy prime minister, Hassan al-Tuhami, to meet secretly with Israeli foreign minister Moshe Dayan in Morocco.

According to Carter, Sadat told him privately during a visit to the White House in April 1977, "I'll even be willing to sign a peace treaty with them." Carter kept that to himself. He never told Brzezinski. He never told Vance. He never told anyone in his administration that this was a promise that had been made to him. No one but Carter could conceive that Sadat would make such a dramatic move as going to Jerusalem.

The second judgment was that the multilateral negotiating process underway in Geneva would drag on and ultimately end unsatisfactorily. Sadat said in April 1978,

> The road to Geneva got lost amongst all the papers. . . . Had we continued to discuss going to Geneva or any other country, the shape of the table we would sit around, whether there would be one or more tables, the flag under which we would sit, and the form of the Arab delegations, all these things would have taken a long time, without us achieving a single solution.[2]

Sadat went to Jerusalem to move the process forward.

Sadat also wanted to avoid negotiating a settlement in Geneva. He did not mind *thinking* about going to Geneva, and he did not mind *thinking* about a comprehensive peace. But by August or September 1977, when he had already tested the waters secretly with Israeli leaders, he began to develop the notion that the time had come for him to take his destiny back into his own hands.

Part of Sadat's reservations about going to Geneva or about advancing a comprehensive peace arose from his determination that Syria was a major obstacle. He did not like Carter's visit with Syrian president Hafiz al-Asad in May 1977, during which the concept of a joint Arab delegation to a Geneva-type conference was seriously discussed. He did not like the fact that, in September 1977, the United States was spending an

---

[2]   *FBIS–MENA*, May 3, 1978.

enormous amount of time trying to figure out how to get the Syrians involved and how to untie the troublesome knot of Palestinian representation. Sadat knew that Mustafa Talas had made a speech in October 1977 in which he said that the creation of Israel in Palestine constituted an unprecedented aggression against the Arab nation. Sadat thought the speech was dreadful. Sadat knew that Syria was not about to embrace any kind of serious negotiation with the Israelis; thus, the process of going to a conference with Syria was an obstacle to regaining Sinai for Egypt.

In addition, Sadat did not want to go to a multilateral conference in which the negotiations would center on issues extraneous to Egyptian national interests. Sadat's goal was to have all of Sinai returned expeditiously, and he was not sure he could get that out of multilateral negotiations in Geneva. Nicholas Veliotes, who was at the State Department in the late 1970s and ambassador to Egypt from 1983 to 1986, told me, "Sadat possessed the fundamental and unalterable preference to keep control of all negotiating decisions in Cairo's hands, and not let them fall into the Syrian preference for concerted action by a unified Arab delegation." Sadat did not want Asad involved in detailed negotiations with Israel in 1977 for the very same reason that Asad and Sadat did not tell Jordan's King Hussein about the 1973 war. Sadat did not want Hussein to participate in the diplomatic aftermath of the 1973 war, because he feared that King Hussein's involvement would cause negotiations to get bogged down over issues like the future of the West Bank and Jerusalem, and Sadat would not get back Sinai. Sadat had gone to war to get back Sinai and to harness the United States. Historians now know that Sadat did the same thing in 1977. He did not want to be bound by Syria or the Palestinians or any other Arab interest that would inhibit Egypt's ability to get back Sinai.

Finally, Anwar Sadat understood his strengths and weaknesses in terms of the regional environment. He understood first and foremost the central importance of Egypt in the region. Anwar Sadat was an Egyptian first, and he made no excuses about his national pride. As he became further and further isolated—after his trip to Jerusalem, and after the Camp David Accords, and after the Egyptian–Israeli peace treaty—he was more and more an Egyptian.

According to Ambassador Roy Atherton, people would say to Sadat, "You're going to isolate Egypt in the Arab world if you sign a peace treaty with Israel." Sadat's reaction was, "The Arabs cannot isolate Egypt; they can only isolate themselves." Sadat was confident of his character and confident of Egypt. The correctness of his assessment was proved by the fact that Egypt was isolated officially for only five years, until 1984, and then gradually over the following five years it brought itself back to the Arab world. After all, what was the first Arab country that Yasir Arafat went to when he left Lebanon in 1984? He went to Greece and then to Cairo. He did not go to Syria. He did not go to Jordan. He went to Egypt. Jordan reestablished diplomatic relations with Egypt in 1984. The Arab world needed Egypt, and Anwar Sadat knew that.

Sadat's expectations for the results of his Jerusalem initiative were extraordinary. He really believed that the Israelis were going to give him something unique. He thought that Begin would declare right after Sadat's address to the Knesset, "Because you've done this, because you've recognized us, we're going to withdraw

from all of Sinai." Obviously, it did not happen, and
Sadat was enormously disappointed that the Israelis
never reacted in kind to what Sadat believed to be an
extraordinary act of vision and courage, by going to
Jerusalem. Former National Security Council aide
William B. Quandt told me, "Sadat talked as if, once
he'd broken the psychological barrier, the Israelis will
have no excuse, and that once they have done this, he's
not going to need even the Americans anymore, because
he'd get back all of Sinai." Sadat had inflated
expectations. The reality, of course, was something else.

In addition, there was an asymmetry to the
consequent negotiations—an asymmetry that has not
gone away. Begin and Sadat had different goals. They
both had goals of reaching an understanding that their
countries would not go to war anymore. Egypt wanted
land; Israel wanted a changed psychological outlook.
Israelis wanted to remove the existential fear. Egypt
sought to preserve its dignity and its honor and to have
its land back. Israelis never doubted the legitimacy of
Egypt before the negotiations began. They never
doubted the legitimacy of Egypt after negotiations
ended. But according to Israelis, Egyptians still
continued to doubt Israel's legitimacy. And those
asymmetrical viewpoints have not yet disappeared.

Egypt—and particularly Sadat—saw all of this.
Sadat saw the negotiations as a series of phases, a series
of steps by which Sinai would be returned to his control,
by which Egypt would lead the Arab world, by which a
comprehensive peace would be achieved and eventually
the territories taken in 1967 would be returned to Arab
control. The Middle East is in the midst of what he saw.
He knew that he would prove to be the catalyst by way
of his trip to Jerusalem.

Discussion

Question: *In a letter Sadat sent to President Carter in 1977, he suggested a summit meeting of the UN Security Council in Jerusalem, also attended by the Egyptians and the Israelis. What happened to this idea, what was the American reaction, and why do you think President Sadat made this suggestion before he put forth the idea of a visit to Jerusalem?*

Eilts: Sadat was exploring all possibilities. As I noted, he was becoming increasingly desperate as 1977 went along. Carter sent Sadat a letter asking for some dramatic effort, and the idea described was one that occurred to Sadat.

We thought it was a lousy idea. Jerusalem, we always recognized, would be one of the most difficult nuts to crack. The Security Council had been unable to do much on peace in general in the preceding years, and we thought giving it the hardest problem to work on was a nonstarter. We threw cold water on that idea from the beginning.

Ben Elissar: On another point. First of all, I agree absolutely with Ambassador Eilts that Sadat wanted a conference in Geneva. The Israelis heard this through the Americans several times.

A point on the United States: The parties that met in Morocco, namely, Tuhami and Dayan, agreed not to inform the Americans. This was on the initiative of the Moroccan king, who told them, "Leave the Americans out of this. We cannot trust them. When you reach an agreement, you will inform the Americans."

So what happened? Begin immediately gave
instructions to inform the Americans, because he did not
trust the Egyptians. Sadat did precisely the same. He
instructed his ambassador here in Washington
immediately to inform the Americans, because he did
not trust Begin.

Eilts: May I just add a point to that? Sadat told the U.S.
government about it, but he said, "Nothing has come out
of these things." I have to say something: One does not
send the court jester—which Tuhami was regarded as
being, in Egyptian thinking—for important discussions.
Sadat liked Tuhami personally, but he would shake his
head about Tuhami. Tuhami came back from Morocco
saying, "I've gotten Jerusalem for you." Even Sadat
recognized that this was not likely to happen.

One additional point here, on a slightly different
matter: I understood the allegation that Dayan promised
the return of all of Sinai differently than it has been
presented. Sadat told me that Ezer Weizman had
confided that he, Ezer, had told Begin, "We do not need
the Sinai settlements for security reasons." Having heard
that, Sadat was convinced that Israel would be willing to
give up the Sinai settlements. Sadat was disillusioned on
the tenth day of the Camp David conference when, after
much urging and pressure, he agreed to meet with
Moshe Dayan again. I have already indicated his
changed view on Dayan. Dayan said, "If anybody told
you that any Israeli government could give up the Sinai
settlements, they were deluding you." Carter had been
trying to persuade Sadat to allow the Sinai settlements to
remain, in the first ten days of the conference; if not
under Israel Defense Force protection, then under UN
protection, or, if necessary, Egyptian protection. Sadat

was very close to Carter and did almost anything that Carter wanted, but on this, he balked.

He gave three reasons for balking: One, he said, "Sinai was the scene of our great defeat. Neither the Egyptian military, nor the Egyptian public, would understand if I agreed that the settlements were to remain." As he put it to me once, "Sinai has to be cleansed of Israelis."

Two, he said, "I know what they are after. They want to set a precedent for their future negotiations with Jordan and with Syria. They want to be able to say, 'Egypt has agreed to the retention of some of the settlements,' but I am not going to give it to them."

But the third was more important to him. He said to President Carter, "Mr. President, you have been pressing upon me that, as part of peace, there must be normalization of relations—diplomatic relations and everything else. Let's face it, Mr. President. If those settlements remain, sooner or later there will be disputes between the settlers and the Egyptian authorities, and it will hurt the cause of normalization. On that, Mr. President, I cannot agree."

Question: *I have heard a story many times from a source that I consider to be very well-connected in Israel. The story goes that before the Sadat visit, Moshe Dayan said, "If I have to choose between peace and keeping Sharm al-Shaykh, I will keep Sharm al-Shaykh."*

Is this accurate, and if so, what caused Dayan to change his mind?

Ben Elissar: It is correct, except that the declaration was made long before Sadat's visit to Jerusalem, perhaps in 1974.

Joseph Sisco, former under secretary of state: Dayan made that statement to me directly. President Sadat signaled to us that he wanted a disengagement agreement. I had a full discussion on this with Dayan, and it was at that particular point that he made the statement.

Ben Elissar: Moshe Dayan obviously changed his attitude at Camp David, when he saw that Israel could not have both peace and Sharm al-Shaykh. Prime Minister Begin also had to change his position on the settlements. He knew that Israel could not have both the settlements in Sinai and those in the West Bank. He had to choose, and he chose.

Question: *Every time the story of Sadat's trip is discussed, there is talk of psychohistory and personalities and motives. Is there any possibility, however, that Sadat was just bluffing, and he was taken by surprise by the Israelis' acceptance of his gesture? Could it be that he just wanted to show peace, and he was stunned to find it was accepted, and then the peace process gained its own life and went on by inertia?*

Eilts: I do not think so. Having been involved almost every day in the period leading up to Sadat's visit, he was not bluffing. He was desperate. Peace was, as he put it, slipping through his fingers because of procedural reasons having to do largely with the Syrians.

The Syrians never said no, by the way, to the U.S. suggestion that they go to Geneva without an agenda; they simply did not reply. Things went on and on and on, and Sadat, especially in response to that Carter letter, came up with the Jerusalem visit.

three

Sadat and the Transformation of Egyptian National Security

Ahmed Fakhr
Wat Cluverius
Kenneth Pollack

Anwar Sadat's decision to make peace with Israel resulted in far-reaching changes in the Egyptian military. Long-accustomed to being on a war footing with its neighbor to the east, the Egyptian military shifted its sights toward maintaining peace. A veteran of many of those changes, Maj. Gen. (ret.) Ahmed Fakhr, analyzes their effects on the Egyptian military. Amb. Wat Cluverius, the director general of the Multinational Force and Observers in Sinai, draws lessons from his close observation of Egyptian–Israeli peacekeeping operations, and military analyst Kenneth Pollack assesses Sadat as one of the greatest military strategists of the modern era.

Ahmed Fakhr

Anwar Sadat is legendary in Egyptian military circles for several reasons. Among them was his decision, as Egypt's supreme commander, to go to war in October 1973 to liberate the largest possible part of the occupied Egyptian territory in the Sinai. It was a bold decision, and one made despite the statement of military détente announced by the United States and the Soviet Union in 1972. This decision gave the military quarters in Egypt the feeling that the supreme commander was capable of defying those stronger than himself.

President Sadat decided to go to war in 1973 despite hearing his commanders project 30,000 Egyptian casualties in the first six hours of the crossing of the canal. He made a calculated risk on the basis of cost–benefit analysis. He earned additional respect because of his successful strategic deception plan prior to crossing the canal. He not only deceived powerful foreign intelligence agencies, but also world public opinion, Egyptian public opinion, and indeed some segment of the Egyptian armed forces itself. I knew about the war only on the October 4, two days before it began.

As a result of his conduct in 1973 and during other moments of great challenge, President Sadat enjoyed a great deal of credibility among the Egyptian military. They believed him and believed in him and thus were highly responsive to the changes he introduced to the concept of Egyptian national security.

Sadat reoriented Egyptian national security along three fronts: weaponry, threat definition, and a redefinition of vital national interests. With regard to the

first, Sadat made a geopolitical decision to ally Egypt
with the Western rather than Eastern Bloc. That decision
called upon the armed forces to phase out Soviet
equipment acquired over the previous twenty years and
simultaneously obtain armaments from an array of other,
mainly Western, countries. Sadat's decision drastically
altered standing military cooperation agreements in
addition to Egypt's political and economic alliances.

His move changed the military frame of mind. This
was in part because the replacement of Soviet materiel
with Western, and principally American, armaments,
also allowed Egypt to reduce the size of its standing
forces. Many of the American weapons systems required
fewer troops to deploy them. I am a SAM-2 officer, and
the army required some hundreds of troops to prepare,
transport, and launch one surface-to-air missile. The
SAM-2's were replaced by American-made HAWK
missiles, whose personnel requirement is only a tenth as
much. In addition, a joint Egyptian–U.S. commission
was established to implement the phasing out of Soviet
equipment and the deployment of U.S. replacement
equipment. A great cooperative spirit grew out of that
work together.

Sadat also radically changed the Egyptian military's
threat definitions. The Egyptian military understood the
declaration that October 1973 would be "the last war" to
mean that all parties in the region renounced the use of
force for solving any political problems relating to the
Arab–Israeli conflict. The Egyptian military believed in
what its president stated, and acted accordingly.

Before Camp David, all Egyptian documents, maps,
directions for training exercises, maneuvers, and
intelligence reports referred to Israel as the enemy.
During the period dominated by the perception of Israel

as the enemy, Egyptian military thought was based on the principle of threat assessment and threat perception. This meant that the Egyptian defense policy was formulated on the basis of close scrutiny of the military and political intentions of Israel and the development of its military and combat capabilities. The assessment of the maximum risk Egypt could face from an Israeli offensive action, as well as the minimum risk that could result from such action, determined Egypt's military needs. These needs include the size and structure of the armed forces, the reserves, and the quantity and quality of weapon systems. This, in turn, determined the amount of military expenditure necessary to build a deterrent defensive military force—one capable of taking appropriate military action should deterrence fail.

After Camp David, a major shift occurred in the basic premise of Egyptian national security thought. According to Sadat's national security doctrine, the primary responsibility of the armed forces was to defend the territory, air space, and territorial waters of Egypt, regardless of whom the aggressors might be. As a consequence, Egyptian military thinking no longer focuses solely on Israel, in the strategic northeastern direction; it now covers all directions. Examples of this change are the clashes on the western border with Libya and the military situation between Egypt and Sudan on the southern border. The "Badr" exercises in 1996, which some criticized, were meant to show the Egyptian armed forces that they may face four attacks from four different directions, from the north, from the south, from the east, and from the west, and they may have to maneuver to repel all of them. The exercises were meant to prepare the armed forces for a worst-case scenario. There was no other motive.

Before his peace initiative, President Sadat introduced a number of small but significant steps that paved the way for the major changes he later introduced. In the months before his trip to Jerusalem, he directed that Egyptian officers be sent to study courses in Western countries, such as the United States, Britain, and France. The courses were attended by officers of various nationalities, including Israelis. The aim was to establish direct contact between the officers of both countries, because such contacts as the first and second disengagement agreements of 1974 and 1975, as well as the joint Egyptian–Israeli patrols, had proven successful. I, myself, did a course in London in 1977, before Sadat's visit to Jerusalem. My classmate was the late Israeli general, Ari Brown, the aide of the late Defense Minister Moshe Dayan. Brown and I stayed together for a whole year with our families.

The participation of Egyptian officers on active duty in international conferences and symposia organized by research centers around the world, and with the participation of Israeli officers, was aimed at promoting mutual trust and common understanding. During the same period, President Sadat accepted delegations of Jewish groups from the United States and Europe in the Egyptian military educational institutions. During my tenure as the commander of the Nasser Higher Military Academy, I was visited by representatives of B'nai B'rith and some members of the American Israel Public Affairs Committee (AIPAC). This was a development whose significance, both psychologically and practically, cannot be underestimated.

President Sadat understood that national security is not based on military factors alone; rather, it is the sum total of the interactions of political, economic, social, and democratic factors and their influence on the decision-making process. "Military action," as he told us, "should not be ruled out, if Egypt's national security is threatened, regardless of the source of that threat. Yet, the interest in resorting to military action must not be permitted to overrule the diplomacy of avoidance of war." Egyptian military circles understood this to mean that parties concerned will do their utmost not to escalate any crisis or dispute to the level of military confrontation or the use of military instruments. This led to the adoption of defensive military policies.

As mentioned above, Egypt's worst-case scenario is to be subjected to simultaneous attacks from all directions. The country's strategic directions are the Mediterranean to the north; to the west, Libya and Chad; Sudan to the south; and Sinai and the Red Sea to the east. The best-case scenario would be for aggression to come from a single direction, while political and diplomatic action secures the other three. Striking a balance between the need to face each scenario is the force governing Egyptian national security thought.

Because under Sadat's thinking Egyptian national security no longer depended entirely on the military actions of one party, Egyptian strategic thinking now identifies the defense of Egyptian vital interests as its basic premise. Military thought makes a distinction between, on the one hand, the national interests, which are protected by the state using all available political, diplomatic, economic, and cultural means, and on the other hand, the vital interests pertaining to the survival and integrity of the state. The defense and the protection of those interests, when subjected to a grave military threat, necessitate the use of military force. When the protection of vital interests replaced threat assessment as the basic premise of national security, the military defined those vital interests as follows: the acquisition of necessary military force to maintain the peace and stability of the region as a whole; the acquisition of the necessary political clout to enlarge the peace circle; the protection of the flow of Nile water from the upstream countries, in accordance with the established international agreement in force; and the protection of free passage—civilian and military—from the Mediterranean, through the Suez Canal, down the Red Sea, and through Bab al-Mandab.

The order of priority of those Egyptian vital interests has not remained static. The accumulation of events has changed some of these priorities, and it is a dynamic change. Egypt now looks toward Iraq to see what will happen in the Gulf. During October 1997, there was some attempt from the Libyan leadership to have millions of Libyans march to demand unity between Egypt and Libya. Such moves could create chaos and are a threat to Egyptian interests, which are dynamic.

The strained relations between Egypt and Sudan, and even Iran, have affected the perception of the protection of Egyptian vital interests, both within and outside Egypt's borders. This makes necessary a revision of the shape and structure of the Egyptian armed forces, particularly in light of Egypt's need for air lift and sea lift capabilities during its military's participation in the international coalition for the liberation of Kuwait. Egypt had to hire Soviet planes and Soviet vessels to transport its troops to the Gulf to join the coalition; it does not have enough on its own.

Finally, broadening conceptions of Egyptian national security have introduced new elements to Egyptian strategic thinking. The open-door policy and its subsequent program of privatization compelled the armed forces to take into account the economic dimensions of defense, a notion that was absent from the Egyptian military thought throughout the period of the Egypt–Israel wars. The resulting shift of emphasis to deterrent defense capability led to a change in the volume and the priorities of the type of weapon systems to be acquired by the Egyptian armed forces. It also led to the establishment of a national service organ to meet the logistical needs of the army away from the civilian market. Strategic needs have also shaped thinking about Egypt's civilian infrastructure. During the October War, when Egypt mobilized its reserve, the military had more than half a million persons in the Cairo railway station. Everyone had to pass through Cairo to get anywhere in the country. The Egyptian military maintains a large reserve force to keep the standing forces at a limited size, and this requires Egypt to have the infrastructure necessary for mobilization, including but not limited to roads, railways, waterways and communications systems. The civilian benefits of using many of these assets during peacetime are obvious.

Sadat saw the interaction of not only the military and the economy but also the military and democracy. At a time when the armed forces were the major players in the decision-making process, President Sadat issued a directive barring the military from political activities, banning its participation in municipal, parliamentary, or upper-house elections. When I was in active service and could vote, the ballot boxes were placed in military barracks and units. Commanders instructed their units how to vote; as a consequence, military officers had a real impact on who would serve in the parliament and even in municipal government. Sadat took the military out of politics, thus putting the armed forces in its proper place in a state moving toward democratization, a multiparty system, a market economy, and civil society. This state of affairs remains unchanged today and is being consolidated every day.

When Anwar Sadat signed the Camp David Accords, his main purpose was to provide a framework for the solution of the Palestinian question, the crux of the Arab–Israeli conflict. The Egyptian military viewed the Madrid conference as an extension and expansion of the Camp David process, to include all parties, with a view to establishing the comprehensive peace President Sadat had spoken so much about.

The policies and actions of President Sadat introduced far-reaching changes in the concept of Egyptian national security. Part of those changes was because of the exchange of promises between President Sadat and the military. He promised the military peace, and he brought peace. The military promised him that it would preserve the peace. We both kept our promises.

Wat Cluverius

The Sinai Peninsula was the territorial manifestation of the Arab–Israeli conflict on the Egyptian–Israeli front. For Egypt, peace would have been unthinkable without the return of the Sinai. For Israel, letting the Sinai revert to Egypt without its demilitarization would have been unthinkable. The Sinai was the closest thing to strategic depth Israel had on any of its borders. As we know, Egypt regained the Sinai, and Israel gained a buffer. The treaty of peace contained security elements which both Israel and Egypt saw then, and now, as critical elements of national security.

To offer this essential demilitarization element to Israel, without which there could have been no peace and no return of the Sinai, President Anwar Sadat relinquished the military expression of Egyptian sovereignty over the Sinai. He agreed to maintain only a limited military presence in a zone just east of the Suez Canal and along the Gulf of Suez. The treaty of peace also limits Israeli operations in a narrow zone on the eastern side of the border.

The present security arrangements involved significant Egyptian concessions in 1979, and Sadat's advisers probably objected to some of them at the time. Even then, Sadat may have been looking beyond the military limitations to the possiblity of developing Sinai to such a degree it would be not only a great strategic asset to Egypt, but also a symbol of peace; and perhaps, if peace should fail, a developed and well-populated Sinai would be just as indigestible to an invader as is Egypt proper.

Did Sadat see all of this, looking ahead at the time? I have no way of knowing. Foreseen or not, it is what is happening to Sinai. This historic invasion route is becoming more developed, more heavily populated, and better served by government. It is doing so by leaps and bounds.

I will return to Sinai's development below, but I will now turn to the formalities of security in the Sinai. The Treaty of Peace called for the United Nations to assume the monetary and security provisions regarding the demilitarization of the Sinai. Two years after the signing of the treaty, it became clear that the threat of a Soviet veto in the UN Security Council would make that impossible. This had been foreseen, and U.S. president Jimmy Carter had assured both President Sadat and Israeli prime minister Menachem Begin that if the UN could not take up the role of monitoring the security aspects of the treaty, the United States would make its best efforts to find an alternative multinational force.

In May 1981, the president of the Security Council informed the members that the UN could not provide the force called for in the treaty. By August 1981, the United States, Egypt, and Israel had negotiated a protocol to the treaty, creating the Multinational Force and Observers (MFO) as a substitute. It was created on paper in August 1981, and it had to be operational at the end of April 1982, the scheduled date for full Israeli withdrawal from the Sinai.

In creating the MFO, the parties and the United States invented a new peacekeeping mechanism in which the parties themselves sit on the "board of directors." It is a mechanism in which both parties have an intimate, day-to-day interest. As a result, over time it has become a mechanism in which the parties can place considerable trust, and they do.

An intense effort by the United States and by the parties soon brought eleven countries to join the MFO. At the time, the British would not have participated had it not been for the personal relationship between Prime Minister Margaret Thatcher and President Ronald Reagan. The Arabs who were opposed to the treaty between Egypt and Israel were pressing their British friends to stay out of this. Thatcher agreed with Reagan, against the advice, I am sure, of the Foreign Office, and certainly of the Ministry of Defense. But she added, "We cannot have the headquarters in London."

The Swiss were afraid that they might be approached to have the headquarters of the MFO in Switzerland, with all those UN organizations there, and they used a back channel to say, "Don't even think about it." The French volunteered to participate but also said, very politely, "Paris is really too far from the scene to host a headquarters." The Italians volunteered to participate in the MFO and said, "By the way, do you need a site for a headquarters?" That is why I sit happily in Rome.

The MFO has worked out very well. It has had enormous continuity of participation. Of the original eleven countries that took up the mission in 1982, only three have left: the United Kingdom, Netherlands, and Australia; and the Australians have returned. That remarkable statement of international commitment to Middle East peace is very important.

There are some unique elements to this MFO that are worth mentioning. The funding for the MFO comes equally from the United States, Israel, and Egypt, with a few symbolic dollars from the Germans, the Japanese, and the Swiss. Egypt and Israel look at management issues in a special way because it is their money. Continuous and ongoing discussions about management is one of the things that increases the trust that the parties have in the organization. They are involved with the MFO day-to-day, not just on the operational mission, but on the management mission.

The MFO's mandate is open-ended. No formal renewal is needed. This fact makes the parties confident that the political passions of any given moment will not disrupt the operation of the peace monitoring. This is not to say that the organization is static. It constantly reviews what is going on in the MFO, and it has made many changes over the years.

The structure of the Rome headquarters is all civilian. It handles diplomacy, funding, legal affairs, and similar matters. I and my headquarters staff basically work for the governments of Egypt and Israel. I was "suggested," as the language of the relevant documents puts it, by the United States. Only the Egyptians and Israelis together can dismiss the director general of the MFO.

I nominate the force commander to Egypt and Israel. Once they agree to him, only I can fire him; they cannot. The person in my job has to be an American, and the force commander cannot be. These are examples of the checks and balances throughout the system.

The MFO has outside auditors, because if it had Israeli standards of auditing, American standards of auditing, and Egyptian standards of auditing, it would never get anything done during the year except prepare for the auditors to arrive in the controller's office. It uses commercial standards and engages one of the large international accounting firms.

The MFO is totally integrated. That means that it does not have a separate Fijian camp and a separate Australian camp. It has combined dining facilities. The MFO owns everything except its ten American helicopters, three Italian coastal patrol boats, and one French fixed-wing aircraft. As a consequence, it has total interoperability of equipment and standardization. This helps promote cost-effectiveness.

The monitoring operations of the MFO are quite repetitious. There has never been a serious violation of this treaty by either side. This is not a tribute to the MFO; this is a tribute to the commitment of both parties to their peace.

One of the most important elements of the MFO's operating environment is the existence, mandated in the treaty, of a liaison system on both sides. The treaty mandated Israel and Egypt to deal with each other on a daily basis, at the borders, on mutual problems. It is absolutely the *sine qua non* of daily success for the MFO. In a period of political tensions, it is the conscious, pursued policy of both sides to keep those tensions from affecting the day-to-day functioning of the liaison systems.

There is an operational tempo here, born partly out of habit, but also out of trying to make this thing work. There is a great deal of understanding and friendship between the officers on both sides. In fact, I would advise anybody negotiating any kind of treaty or agreement, in a situation that has had as many decades of hostilities as this one has, to mandate a liaison system. It would be much better if they had mandated a liaison system on the Golan Heights with the United Nations Disengagement Observer Force (UNDOF), so the

Israelis and Syrians would have to talk to each other. Talking helps. It makes a big difference.

The Sinai is a tremendous economic asset to Egypt, and I think that also makes it something of a symbol of peace. Nothing so indicates Egypt's peaceful intentions in Sinai as its rapid population of the area, its investments in Sinai, and Sinai's integration into the rest of the country.

Egypt has made a symbol out of Sinai. If the Israelis are watching Sinai, as I know they are, to see whether Egypt repopulated it with soldiers or farmers, then Sinai has become a symbol of peace. It is a statement that Sinai is not only an amazingly beautiful place, but it is also a symbol of peace. What the Egyptian government has done with it is extraordinary.

The most logical question I get from any audience is, if all is going so well in the Sinai, when can the MFO pack up and leave? The short answer is, when both parties jointly wish it to pack up and go, it will go. It is their treaty, and the MFO is their instrument. My sense is that they might wish to forgo the MFO when the wider neighborhood, including Syria, Lebanon, the Palestinians, enjoy the beginnings of the same peace that my 2,000 young soldiers in the Sinai see every day. That is when the confidence-building presence that the MFO represents will no longer be needed, because the circle of peace will have been closed.

Kenneth Pollack

President Anwar Sadat quite rightly gets a great deal of praise for the courage and the vision that he showed in making peace with Israel. But what gets lost in the glare of that spotlight is the skill, savvy, and insight that he brought, as a war leader and as a statesman. The only company that one can put him in is that of other great war leaders like Winston Churchill, Abraham Lincoln, and Franklin Roosevelt.

Anwar Sadat fundamentally transformed the Egyptian military, and he did it in every manner imaginable. The Egyptian military was demoralized in 1970. It was politicized. It lacked any real doctrine or sense of an operational concept. It did not really know what it was doing. Anwar Sadat transformed the Egyptian military into a force capable of executing Egyptian foreign policy and capable of accomplishing goals for the country. Sadat greatly expanded the professionalization of the Egyptian military. He took the Egyptian military out of politics, and he took the politics out of the Egyptian military. He brought in a team of superb generals—Ahmad Ismail 'Ali, Saad al-Din Shazli, Muhammad Abdel Ghani al-Gamassy—to recreate the Egyptian military and to turn it into a real force that could execute the foreign policy that he had in mind. These men then turned around and gave Egypt an operational concept. It was because of the operational concept that Ismail 'Ali, Shazli, Gamassy, and others brought, and which Sadat encouraged them to bring, that Egypt was able to accomplish its goal.

In addition, Sadat artfully used limited warfare as an aspect of foreign policy. Sadat's approach to the

problem of Egypt's relationship to Israel was sheer
genius. He decided that he would make war so that he
could make peace. It is very hard, in modern history, to
find other examples of a leader who could think along
those lines. What is more, he did not put forth the simple
proposition that he was going to make war to get peace
eventually. He made war to convince the United
States—a third party—to get involved in the conflict and
to intervene with the Israelis. What is more, he
recognized that all he needed to do was to get across the
Suez Canal; he did not have to reconquer Sinai.

The traditional method of using limited war is to
capture a defined piece of land, hang onto it, and then
fight one's opponent to a standstill. That is essentially
what the Israelis did in 1967. The tradition goes back to
Frederick the Great when he grabbed Silesia in 1743.
Sadat broke the mold completely, and he did so against
the advice of many of his generals. He did so in a way
that stunned the rest of the world. No one could imagine
that one could grab a tiny sliver of territory and then
negotiate the handover of an area many multiples of
times larger, but Sadat did it.

It is stunning, first of all, that Sadat could even think
along these lines. What is even more amazing is that
Sadat actually made this work. Bureaucracies do not
favor very subtle, sophisticated, complicated goals.
Sadat's Sinai strategy was about as sophisticated and
convoluted as possible. If President Bill Clinton walked
into the Pentagon, occupied by the most powerful
military the world has ever seen, and said, "I want to do
something like this," the chairman of the Joint Chiefs of
Staff, Gen. Hugh Shelton, would laugh at him. He would
say, "We cannot do that. That is not what militaries do."
Yet, Sadat did it, and he made it work. He found

generals who could do it. He managed to formulate a strategy and then implement it, which entirely transformed both Egypt's security situation and the larger Middle East.

Sadat, in this transformation of Egyptian national security, took everything that the Germans were able to do in about fifty years, and he did it in three. The professionalization that Sadat began in the Egyptian military was along the lines of the reforms that G. J. D. von Scharnhorst began in 1807. The operational concept that he developed, along with Ismail 'Ali, Shazli, and Gamassy, was akin to the reforms that Helmut von Moltke was executing in the 1860s. Finally, the only thing I can think of that even comes close to his limited war strategy is what Chancellor Otto von Bismarck accomplished in the 1860s and 1870s. What is more, thinking over what Bismarck was able to accomplish as opposed to what Sadat conceptualized and was able to accomplish, Sadat may actually get the higher marks of the two.

I would like to add a quick word about the impact of Sadat's transformation of Egyptian national security on the transformation of U.S. national security. Right now, in 1997, there are obvious strains in the peace process, and there are also obvious strains in the U.S. relationship with Egypt, in part related to the strains in the peace process. Evident tensions have led to a great deal of pessimism about where the relationship is going. In point of fact, however, I think that there is a great deal of hope and strength in the U.S.–Egyptian military relationship. On the military-to-military side, which is something that Anwar Sadat began, ties are tremendously strong between the two countries, and they get stronger and stronger every day.

The strong military-to-military relationship is a great asset to both sides. It is worth remembering when policymakers think about the way that the United States conducts its policy in the Middle East, and all of the power and influence that the United States can bring to bear in the Middle East, that much of that power is, directly or indirectly, a result of America's relationship with Egypt and with the Egyptian military. Almost any time there is a crisis in the world and the United States needs to move something somewhere fast, it goes through Egypt. Whether it is a carrier going to the Gulf, troops crossing Egyptian airspace, or transport aircraft staging out of Egyptian air bases, the United States cannot defend the Persian Gulf without Egypt.

What is more, Egyptians contribute directly to America's military strength. It was so important to have Egyptian troops with U.S. troops in Bosnia. It was so important to have Egyptian troops with U.S. troops in Somalia. And it was absolutely essential that Egyptian troops participated with U.S. troops in the Gulf.

The military-to-military relationship is very strong. The United States must continue to strengthen it, and be sure to recognize the importance and the role of that relationship in the larger U.S. policy toward the region.

Discussion

Question: *How is it that the Egyptian military went from being one of the most vocal opponents of peace with Israel to being the greatest proponent of peace and stability in the region? Can Egypt's lessons be applied to other armies in the region?*

Fakhr: It starts politically. President Sadat's first step was to change the title of the Ministry of War to the Ministry of Defense. Down the chain of command, the military shifted from an offensive to a defensive posture.

Second, personal relations have made a big difference, especially between the U.S. military and the Egyptian military. The Soviets were in Egypt for fifteen years. They penetrated every segment of Egypt's society—all the way from folkloric dance troupes, to military advisers, to theater groups, to the press—but Egyptians called them a society of the third person. One could not talk to a Russian without having somebody along to listen and report. The Soviets trained the Egyptian military, and they improved its knowledge about war and about force structure. They were helpful according to the contracts in general, but they were task-oriented rather than knowledge-oriented people. When they were expelled from the country, nobody was sorry, because Egyptians had no real friendship with them. I never went to a house where a Soviet expert lived. I was never able to invite a Soviet expert to my house.

Go now to any Egyptian airbase, where U.S. F-16 pilots are; go to West Cairo Airport; go to where the M-1 tanks are built; see how the Americans and the Egyptians are interacting. U.S. officers will visit their military chauffeur, a private, in a small village if he is sick. There are personal relationships. Personal relations are the basis for confidence-building between two sides once both agree that they share the same objective of a comprehensive peace, despite any political differences that might exist.

Equally important, seeing is believing, especially to the military. If the U.S. government generously offers a grant for a sewage project in Cairo, a citizen in Cairo will still suffer from inadequate sewers for ten to twelve years until the project is completed. During that period, the Americans will complain that they are putting money in the aid pipeline which is not being spent.

But in the military, if the U.S. government promises an F-16, the pilot gets the F-16. Washington promises an armored personnel carrier, and here is the armored personnel carrier; with a HAWK missile, here is the HAWK missile. That is why the credibility is stronger. It is not a statement of diplomats, with commas and semicolons, or an agreement to take a matter under consideration.

With regard to other Arab countries, if they can reach agreements with Israel, I do not believe that they will be any less committed to peace than the Egyptians have been. I still lecture in all the military educational institutions, including the Nasser Higher Military Academy, at least once a month. Officers from all the Arab countries attend our courses, and they listen to Egyptians discuss their experience in Sinai, their experience with the Multinational Force and Observers (MFO) liaison committees, their experience with confidence-building measures, and their experience with Americans.

It is not a question of optimism or pessimism. Soldiers anywhere understand what war means. Perhaps the diplomat understands peace better than does the soldier, but the soldier understands war better. I am sure that once a political decision is made on peace, the militaries will follow quickly behind. The commitment to peace will increase as a consequence of military involvement.

Question: *Other than your suggestion about the importance of direct liaison functions in maintaining a peace, what other advice would you give future peacekeeping missions?*

Cluverius: For one thing, one must remember that the MFO is in the service of a treaty of peace. It does not protect an armistice, and it does not protect a demilitarized zone (DMZ). The difference between a peace treaty and a disengagement agreement is that the former is a commitment of a government and people, and the latter is a temporary commitment of the generals in the field or of a few diplomats.

I think the MFO model has some use, not just for the future in the Middle East, but for any place that still needs a confidence-building presence. The liaison system is the key to this, in my view. No matter how many hundreds of years of conflict the parties have behind them, they should be mandated to meet on a regular basis and solve problems. Do not let them go only through the UN or some other structure. They should be forced to meet.

The mere existence of meetings affects the culture. If you put a lot of sergeants together, the drivers get to know each other, the corporals get to know each other, and so on. They may not like each other at the beginning, but I have seen very few cases where there were any really strong animosities after a lengthy period of association. One side may not like the other, but each will know the other is human.

Question: *General Fakhr, how does the Egyptian military feel about the fact that part of this peace denies Egypt military sovereignty over a large piece of its territory?*

Fakhr: The Egyptian military has no concerns about the Camp David military arrangements. It has a zone that is completely demilitarized, a zone with limited guard troops, and then a zone with a specified number of tanks and infantry and artillery. During the hostilities between Egypt and Israel, Egypt never had more than one infantry division in Sinai. It was there merely for reconnaissance, to buy some time for the main troops to cross the Suez Canal and come from the West to Sinai. The desert is too difficult a climate in which to station troops and equipment for long periods of time.

From the point of view of the military, there is no problem with the Sinai arrangements. The problem is with the civilians, who criticize the military for conceding too much. As things stand, Israeli troops can reach the Egyptian–Israeli border in seven hours, but it takes Egyptian troops seven days to reach it. The civilians portray this as a catastrophe for Egyptian national security. The civilians do not believe the military when they are told, "Don't worry. We have enough troops in Zone A to give us the alarm. We have a third party who can give them early warning. We have liaison officers, committees, and patrols." The civilians do not believe the military to this very day.

As Ambassador Cluverius described, Sinai has some 50,000 hotel rooms, a network of roads, numerous villages, water, and investors, and they are all under Egyptian sovereignty. Nobody can invest in or build a hotel, or a road, or an airport, or fly a plane to the area by asking Israel for permission. They ask the Egyptian government. Egypt has complete civil sovereignty over Sinai. From our point of view, that is enough, considering that there will be no more wars. It is enough, at least, to buy time if there were to be any aggression, and in that event the military would have its ways.

Cluverius: The MFO has daily contact with the Egyptian military in the Sinai, in Zones A, B, and C. The number of times over the years that the MFO has found any real animosity toward it or its mission is very small.

General Fakhr said that the Egyptians have a division in Zone A. In fact the treaty allows them to have 22,000 troops in Zone A. I do not think the MFO has ever counted more than 8,000 troops in Zone A. If it were considered a military imperative to have a lot of people on the east bank of the canal, then there would be 22,000. Obviously, the Egyptians do not think it is imperative. Civilian complaints about Egypt relinquishing military sovereignty over the Sinai are an emotional response by people who do not understand military tactics.

Question: *We know that after 1967 the Egyptian military began drawing up plans to reconquer Sinai. Could you tell us to what extent Sadat changed the plan that Gamal Abdel Nasser worked out after 1967?*

Fakhr: I will try to recall what happened after the defeat of 1967. I repeat, after the *defeat*, because psychologically, the armed forces were devastated by their quick defeat in 1967. The plans by President Nasser and his staff, at the time, were dependent on the procurement of weapon systems from the Soviet Union. Yet, the Soviets did not have trust and confidence in the Egyptian military. Soviet military advisers said Egypt could not assault the Suez Canal, it could not use ramparts, it could not cross the Bar Lev line. They said that Egypt needed an atomic bomb. This demoralized the Egyptian military.

Yet, Sadat's plan for assaulting the Suez Canal was never presented to Soviet experts. He carried out this plan the same way the Free Officers carried out the revolution in 1952. He selected some eighty officers, gave them different assignments, and had them make the plan very far away from the Soviets. The Soviets were training Egyptians on another, completely different plan.

There was not a single Nasser plan to regain the Sinai. Nasser made many amendments and changes over time. Of course, he hoped to recapture all of Sinai, but when he asked for some types of planes and the Soviets refused, he changed the plans, and the area to be regained by military action was reduced. When Nasser asked for mobile surface-to-air missiles to protect the infantry and the armor and the Soviets would only supply an insufficient number, another change occurred.

Question: *No institution, be it a political institution or a military institution, is uniform. Within any institutions are differences of opinion. General Fakhr, what kinds of division of opinion existed, in September–October 1977, prior to Sadat's visit to Jerusalem?*

Fakhr: Yes, there was a division of opinion among the military, but not because of the visit to Jerusalem. The visit took the Egyptian military by surprise. No one in the military thought that Sadat was really going to Israel. He used to talk to the soldiers, saying "My kids, my boys, I want to save your blood." We believed that. I remember hearing the beating hearts of the soldiers and officers as we watched television in the barracks when Sadat landed at Ben Gurion Airport. We were very worried, but we believed that it would save our blood.

My generation went through four wars: 1956, 1967, the War of Attrition, and the 1973 War. Four wars in one generation is more than enough. We thought Sadat going to Jerusalem was a good step.

After Camp David, however, there was a division. Some officers resigned, others retired. Some officers joined political opposition parties simply because those parties attacked Camp David and the peace with Israel.

They are not the problem. The problem is that during the hostilities, Israel was the threat, and it was given the title of "the enemy." After the peace treaty, in our documents and in our minds, it was changed to "adversary." After the Israeli withdrawal from the Sinai and the success of confidence-building measures there, it became "the neighboring country."

Unfortunately, in lecturing in the military institutions over the last nineteen months, I discovered that Israel has become "the unpredictable next-door neighbor." These are exactly the words I heard from the Egyptian military at the Nasser Higher Military Academy a month ago. As the military sees it, if Israel is talking about taking back Hebron or Gaza, what will stop them from taking back Sinai? There is a real sense of concern in Egyptian quarters these days.

four

Sadat's Strategy and Legacy

Shimon Shamir
Saad Eddin Ibrahim
Shibley Telhami

Sadat's legacy as the president of Egypt remains the subject of heated debate in Egypt and the rest of the Middle East. Shimon Shamir, a student of modern Egyptian history as well as a former Israeli ambassador to Egypt and Jordan, reviews Sadat's role in moving Egypt away from the problems created by Nasserism and toward a new future. Saad Eddin Ibrahim recounts his private meeting with Sadat just months before Sadat's assassination, and how reflecting on that meeting in later years prompted his own rethinking of Sadat's legacy. Finally, Shibley Telhami, who holds the Anwar Sadat Chair at the University of Maryland, discusses how studying Sadat's actions caused him to rethink many of his assumptions as a political scientist.

Shimon Shamir

Sometime after the assassination of President Anwar Sadat, I was talking to a friend in Cairo who had known Sadat very well and had served as a minister in one of his cabinets, and I asked him for his assessment of the situation. I vividly remember his answer. He said to me, "Try to see Egypt as a car and the president as the driver. Now, the first driver was Nasser. He was an adventurer and a reckless driver and when he died, the car had been badly damaged. It was lying in the ditch, half-buried in the mud. Sadat came, and with a great effort he pulled the car out of the ditch and put it on the road—battered, muddy, but ready to go. Now it is Mubarak's turn to sit at the wheel, take the driver's seat, and start driving ahead."

I relate this story not to make any statement about the role of Mubarak, which is outside the scope of this conference, but simply to point out that it is impossible to evaluate properly Sadat's role and his contribution to his country without relating it to the problems that he had inherited from his predecessor.

I know that the balance sheet of Nasserism is a very controversial matter. In Egypt, as in other countries, thousands of articles and dozens of books have been written on this subject. Nasser definitely had great achievements, albeit mostly in the 1950s, and his impact on the history of the region cannot be denied.

But it is also a matter of consensus among observers of Egyptian affairs and among historians that, by the mid-1960s, the Nasserite revolution had reached an impasse. In almost every field, the revolution was at a dead end and facing problems with which, as it turned

out, it was incapable of coping. This is what Sadat
inherited. I would like to demonstrate this by discussing
five major areas of Egyptian policy. I will examine the
nature of the impasse and how Sadat coped with it.

The first area is that of Egypt's Arab policy.
Arabism was a central element in Nasser's policies and
certainly the main element that supported his claim for
leadership in the region. In 1961, Egypt's union with
Syria collapsed,[1] causing the end of what was called, in
Nasserite ideology, "the unity of ranks." In 1963, a
federation between Egypt, Syria, and Iraq was aborted,
and that was the end of what Nasserites called "the unity
of goals." In 1965–1966, it transpired that a round of
Arab summits—which was presented as "the unity of
action"—were really leading nowhere and were only
exposing the differences among Arabs.

Arabism was draining Egyptian resources, especially
Egypt's policy of military intervention in Yemen's civil
war. In many ways, it turned out that even for supporters
of pan-Arabism, Nasser increasingly seemed a liability
because of the apprehensions and the suspicions that he
generated among other Arab governments. The whole
vision of Arab unity was in crisis in 1970.

Sadat understood that Arabism was probably the
wrong paradigm for coping with the problems of Egypt.
His so-called "October Paper" stated it very clearly.[2] In
Sadat's language, "The era of empty slogans is over." As

---

[1]   In 1958, Egypt and Syria joined to form "The United
Arab Republic." The "northern province," as Syria was called,
withdrew from the union when Egyptian domination proved
too much to bear.

[2]   Issued in April 1974, the October Paper was intended to
capitalize on the "spirit" brought about by Egyptian troops
breaching Israeli defenses during the October 1973 War.

laid out in the October Paper, Sadat sought to reestablish relations with Arab countries on the principle of "interests." This was the key word in the whole document. Sadat believed it was mutual interest that should direct and guide relations between Arab countries, not anything else.

By opting for this approach, Sadat was reasserting the primacy of the Egyptian nation-state. Nasser wiped the name "Egypt" off the map in 1958 when he created the United Arab Republic. Sadat renamed the country the Arab Republic of Egypt, thereby restoring the country's historic legacy.

These days, it is fashionable to speak of the triumph of the territorial state in the Arab world as one of the most remarkable developments of the second half of the twentieth century. It turned out that local interests are too powerful, and even if the political creations of the British and the French were not founded on national or ethnic realities, local interests prevailed. By redefining Egypt's relation to the Arab world on the basis of Egyptian interests, Sadat actually predicted this conclusion, twenty years before the Gulf War showed it to be the dominant principle in the policies of the Arab states.

The second area I would like to examine is that of Egypt's policy toward the great powers, which the vocabulary of Nasserism described as "positive neutrality." Positive neutrality spoke of a new dawn of emerging Third World countries that somehow would separate the two rival superpowers and bring peace to the world. Essentially, however, it was a strategy for playing the two powers against each other to draw as many benefits as possible. Although this was a successful policy for a time, it could not continue indefinitely. The end of that policy can be identified

somewhere in the mid-1960s, when U.S. president
Lyndon Johnson canceled foreign aid to Egypt. Nasser's
people in Washington threatened that they would turn to
the Soviet Union, and Washington told them, "You can
turn to whomever you wish." That was the end of
positive neutrality as an effective strategy.

When Sadat came to power, he noted that although
Nasser liberated Egypt from the presence of tens of
thousands of British troops, when he died a similar
number of Soviet experts, advisers, and military
personnel were stationed there. In 1972, Sadat told the
Soviets to leave. He reoriented Egypt, clearly, toward the
United States.

Did Sadat know, in 1972, that within twenty years
the United States would be the only superpower in the
world? I doubt it. But he certainly sensed that the United
States had a level of influence in the Middle East—and
in other regions—that the Soviet Union lacked, and that
the position of the Soviet Union was waning.

The third area is that of the socioeconomic system.
Here Nasserism proposed "Arab socialism" as a social
and economic system. The 1960–1965 five-year
economic plan started very well, but because of the high
cost of intervention in the Yemeni civil war and other
inadequacies, growth declined sharply. The second five-
year plan, in 1966–1970, was actually terminated within
a year or two. Economic growth at the end of the Nasser
period was actually negative.

Even the revolution's social aspects came into doubt.
In 1966, the Egyptian government proclaimed a "war
against feudalism." In so doing, it implicitly admitted
that feudalism still existed in Egyptian villages more
than a decade after the revolution, and that the social
system had not changed as radically as was assumed.

Sadat sneered at this socialism, although not immediately. He needed Nasserism for a certain period to legitimize his rule. Once he felt confident in his position, he would say things like, "What kind of socialism was that that could not even feed its own people?" He called it "the socialism of poverty" and introduced his own formula: economic openness (*infitah*) and liberalization. Although this policy had only limited success, it did guide Egypt toward a market economy long before the change became universal.

The fourth area is that of the political system. Nasserism established a one-party system and presented it as "true democracy." The resultant series of organizations proved to be neither democratic nor politically effective. To make things worse, most of the people around Nasser who were supposed to be idealistic supporters of the revolution turned out to be power-hungry apparatchiks engaged in internal rivalries and bent on abusing the privileges of power.

Sadat coped with this challenge by proclaiming a "corrective revolution." He eliminated the top echelon of the previous regime and proclaimed what he called a "state of institutions." Of course, there was a gap between the promise and the reality, but it should be admitted that Sadat ushered in political pluralism. It started with the creation of several political "platforms." There was a setback in September 1981, a short time before his assassination, but on the whole, Sadat restored political liberalism to Egypt.

The fifth and last point is the conflict with Israel. Nasser, during most of his rule, correctly evaluated his capabilities and had a realistic strategy toward Israel. His problem was that he blundered into an adventure in 1967 that contradicted most of his past evaluations and ended in a disaster that deeply demoralized the Egyptian people. I would argue that this cannot be separated from his failures in the other four fields. It is because things were going so badly from the mid-1960s that Nasser was ready to gamble on a single card. He hoped that if his move to remilitarize Sinai succeeded, then this would restore his prestige and perhaps the momentum of his revolution in the other fields would be regenerated.

Sadat managed to launch a successful offensive, restore Egyptian pride, and eventually regain the Sinai. By his courageous and visionary move to make peace with Israel, he succeeded in freeing Egypt from the conflict with Israel that had become a formidable burden under Nasser.

Sadat should be credited, then, with reorienting Egypt toward the world of the 1980s, the 1990s, and beyond. He oriented Egypt toward a world of globalism, a world in which economic considerations are primary, a world that has only one superpower, a world in which revolutionary ideologies and fervor are no longer credible. Internally, he oriented Egypt to a system in which economic and political liberalization are vital. To quote Abdul Qader Hatem, minister of information under both Nasser and Sadat, "Sadat simply tried to catch up with the spirit of the times."

Of course, Sadat did not succeed in all his efforts, but perhaps a good definition of what he did manage to do could be expressed in the words of Zulu chief Mangosuthu Buthelezi: "It is true that a march of a thousand miles begins with a single step, but in order to make this single step, you must first face in the right direction." Sadat did precisely that. In some areas, he made progress; in some areas, his progress was limited, but the direction he chose was correct, as can be seen clearly from today's perspective.

To achieve such profound changes, one has to be a remarkable decision maker, and this is indeed what Sadat was. Typical of his decisions is the fact that he tried to avoid half-measures, and he usually followed the rationales of his policies to their logical extremes. Here are a few examples.

In 1973, experts tried to analyze Sadat's military options in view of the constraints on Egyptian capabilities. They usually came up with options that fell short of an all-out war. This was not the Sadat way. Sadat took all five infantry divisions he possessed and threw them across the canal, and his two armored divisions followed. He committed and risked everything he had for a single effort. This was typical of Sadat.

Consider the expulsion of the Soviet personnel. Any political advisor would have told Sadat, "Do it carefully. Try to reduce the number of Soviets gradually. Don't embarrass the Soviet Union; it's a great power." This was not Sadat's way. He made a public announcement and expelled them all in a single move.

The elimination of the Nasserite elite was even more dramatic. Sadat was completely surrounded by "the centers of power"—very powerful people. They controlled the army, the Arab Socialist Union (ASU), the propaganda machinery, and the internal security organizations. He did not try to drive a wedge between them and remove them one by one, as conventional wisdom would have advised. He appointed Mamduh Salem as the interior minister and told him to arrest them all. In one act he eliminated the minister of war, the minister of internal affairs, the heads of the ASU, and many key functionaries.

Finally, what decision is more remarkable than Sadat's decision to conclude full peace with Israel? Other Arab leaders have since opted for peace, but they did so after peace had been legitimized at the Madrid Conference. When Sadat made his decision, peace amounted to a flagrant violation of the Arab consensus. Political prudence would have advised him to opt for secret diplomacy and step-by-step agreements. Instead, Sadat went to Jerusalem and proclaimed to the Knesset his readiness for full peace. This bold act got for him what no half-measures could have achieved.

Sadat was not a particularly modest person and he took great pride in his decision-making capabilities. He would say, in his various speeches and interviews, that he made one major decision every year he was in office. In his language, "In 1971, I eliminated the centers of power; in 1972, I expelled the Soviets; in 1973, I launched the October War; in 1974, I proclaimed the *infitah*; in 1975, I reopened the Suez Canal; in 1976, I reintroduced political pluralism; in 1977, I made my historic trip to Jerusalem; in 1978, I went to Camp David; in 1979, I signed the peace treaty; and in 1980, I cancelled the emergency laws." Nothing was said in 1981, and there must be an explanation for that.

How can this remarkable capacity to make great decisions be explained? Perhaps it would be helpful to refer to the concept of "operational code," developed by Alexander George and others. The concept was quite fashionable in the professional literature years ago, but I think it is still a useful one. Theorists of this approach argue that, to understand decisions, one must refer to a person's belief system. Here are some of the elements that constituted Sadat's belief system.

First, Sadat appears to have truly believed that guidance should be drawn from inside a man's personality, from the depth of his soul. Sadat was a person who made a decision by withdrawal, unlike most other leaders. When others face crucial dilemmas and difficult choices, they often open up to advice from different sides, they invite position papers, and then they try to steer a course that somehow will bring together the various viewpoints and interests.

Sadat made many of his crucial decisions by withdrawing to his village, Mit Abul Kum, separating himself from his advisers and from his government, as he used to put it, so he could "listen to his inner voice." When he emerged with a decision, it was entirely of his own making. He was totally committed to it, he believed in its correctness, and he could follow it through. He did not believe in compromised decisions.

Second, change was a core value for Sadat. Whenever he faced a difficult situation, he saw the possibility of radical change and understood the need for it. Sadat understood that change must begin on the cognitive level. He used to quote a famous Islamic saying: "He who cannot change his thoughts will be unable to change his situation." It reflected Sadat's understanding that—in the language of psychology—change is "dispositional" before it is "situational," and one needs both elements to bring about true change. Among Egyptian intellectuals, some critics of Sadat would say that cognitive change was easier for him because he did not have deep ideological commitments. In many ways this is true, but he turned it to his advantage by accepting change much more easily than the intellectuals around him.

Third, Sadat believed that particular policies should be put in the broad context of a grand strategy. Here are two examples of how it worked—one from the military field and one from diplomacy. The two episodes reflect the wide gap that often existed between Sadat's broad strategy and the narrower perspective of his close aides who focused on immediate gains and losses. Both of these episodes are highly credible, since they come from the memories of those who had experienced confrontations of this kind with Sadat, and years after the events still believed that Sadat was wrong, completely missing the essence of his grand strategy.

General Saad al-Din Shazli, who as chief of staff in the October War bitterly clashed with Sadat, wrote a book in which he explained their differences. His book was designed to show that Sadat was wrong about the conduct of the war, but if one reads the book carefully it proves exactly the opposite.

Shazli asserted that, after the Israelis crossed the Suez Canal in 1973, military logic would have prescribed that forces be withdrawn from the eastern bank of the canal to the western bank to stop the Israeli penetration. Militarily, Shazli was right. But Sadat refused to withdraw a single soldier, telling Shazli, "You do not understand the logic of this war." Sadat, of course, meant that the war had *policy* objectives, and those demanded that every soldier possible remain on the east bank. Shazli became a bitter opponent of Sadat, accusing him of wasting the fruits of the canal crossing. He did not understand that Sadat actually reaped them very nicely.

The other example is from diplomacy. Foreign Minister Ibrahim Kamel clashed with Sadat at Camp David and eventually resigned. In his book he tries to prove how right he was and how wrong Sadat was. He records a conversation between Foreign Ministry Legal Director Nabil el-Araby and Sadat, in which Sadat said:

> Then listen to what I have to say. I heard you out without interrupting you, so nobody can claim . . . that I neither listen nor read! I would like you to know, though, that what you have just been saying has gone into one ear and out of the other!
>
> You people in the Foreign Ministry are under the impression that you understand politics. In reality, however, you understand absolutely nothing. Henceforth I shall not pay the least attention to either your words or your memos. I am a man whose actions are governed by a higher strategy which you are incapable of either perceiving or understanding. I do not need your insignificant and misleading reports.[3]

These are strange words, probably spoken in anger, but they reflect the difference between Sadat's approach and that of his advisers.

Sadat also had a deep belief in his own authority, not a relative authority that emanates from circumstantial political factors, but as a kind of authority that is inherent in his person, similar to the authority enjoyed by a head of a family. He felt he had to be respected because of who he was, not because he was elected in any form or approved by any state institution. He used to refer to himself as *kabir al-a'ilah*, the head of the family. When he faced excessive criticism, he felt that this was shameful, and he named the laws restricting such criticism "the laws of shame."

---

[3]   Mohamed Ibrahim Kamel, *The Camp David Accords: A Testimony* (London: KPI, 1986).

Essentially, Sadat was a traditional person, despite all the radical changes he introduced. He was deeply rooted in his village background. He was also a religious person—his beliefs emphasizing religion *per se*. The broad principles of religion were sometimes more important to Sadat than the particularities of Islam. At one point he said to Edward Sheehan, "I have just finished reading the four gospels of Matthew, Mark, Luke, and John. As a result of my studies, I am going to prove to the world that Islam and Christianity are identical. I shall leave it to the theologians to work out the details."[4]

To conclude, we should of course avoid idealizing and romanticizing Sadat's personality. He had great achievements, and he had great weaknesses. I am not sure that we yet have sufficient perspective to appreciate fully what he did or where he failed.

There have already been a number of reevaluations of Sadat's record, coming up with new perspectives. The most notable of these is perhaps the book written by Saad Eddin Ibrahim, *A Reconsideration of Sadat* (in Arabic). In this book, he reevaluates the policies of Sadat, shifting from rejection to approval, with an intellectual honesty that I deeply admire. There probably will be other reevaluations in the future.

Sadat may have solved problems of which we are not aware now, or he may have created others that have not yet surfaced. "History," said Tolstoy, "is like a deaf man who goes on answering those questions that nobody asks."

---

[4]   Sheehan, *The Arabs, Israelis, and Kissinger: A Secret History of American Diplomacy* (New York: Reader's Digest Books, 1976).

Saad Eddin Ibrahim

I came from a Nasserite background. It took me ten years to appreciate what Anwar Sadat did. This is typical of many intellectuals in Egypt and the Arab world. It probably will take some of them an even longer time than the ten years it took me. It was an agonizing personal journey from being a Nasserite to being an admirer of President Sadat, and it was a wrenching process on the psychological, emotional, and intellectual level.

My journey started on Thursday, August 27, 1981. I got a telephone call. Somebody identified himself as a presidential aide and summoned me to see President Sadat two days hence. I asked this presidential aide, "What is the purpose of the meeting?" He said, "I don't know." "How long is the meeting to be?" He said, "I don't know." "Where is the meeting to be?" He said, "In Alexandria, in the Ma'amoura rest house of President Sadat."

On Saturday morning, the day I was supposed to go, I got up early. My wife and I started looking at the paper, and we found on the front pages of *al-Ahram* and the *Egyptian Gazette* an item in a box in the middle of the page. The item said that President Sadat was in seclusion and not seeing anybody because he was preparing for a big decision and a major speech to the nation that would take place on September 5.

I looked at my wife and told her what I read. What was I supposed to do? Here I was summoned to go and see the president, and now *al-Ahram* says that he is not seeing anybody. Could one of our friends have played a trick on us? She asked me to recall what the voice was like: Ahmed Fakhr, Tahsin Bashir, Osama El-Baz, 'Ali al-Din Hillal—all of our friends who, at that time, could have played that trick.

In her wisdom, my wife said, "He is your president. If he is expecting you and you do not show up, it would be very bad. On the other hand, all it would take is three hours driving to Alexandria and three hours coming back. If he, in fact, is not seeing anybody, that is all that you would have lost: six hours of car driving."

I did go, and I very timidly approached the gates of President Sadat's rest house. At the gate I said very hesitantly, "There was to be a meeting." The guard said, "You are Dr. Saad Eddin Ibrahim?" I said, "Yes, I am." He said, "Yes, we are expecting you." The guard asked me to open the trunk, searched the car, and said, "Drive off until you reach the rest house, and there somebody will tell you what to do." I drove for ten or fifteen minutes in the huge expanse around the rest house in Alexandria.

Finally, I got to the end of the driveway. I got out. I could see President Sadat under an umbrella, looking at the Mediterranean, obviously in a very reflective mood. I proceeded to go to him directly, but somebody immediately appeared and said, "No. First go to the house. Mrs. Jihan Sadat is expecting you."

I was ushered to the rest house. There was Mrs. Sadat, charming as usual. She received me very warmly and served me very cold mango juice and a good Turkish coffee. We chatted.

She told me that she had personally arranged this meeting because, as she said, "The president is not getting honest advice. We need somebody like yourself to tell him, even if bluntly, what is going on in the country. Many of his aides do tell him, but I do not trust their versions. The only one who used to be honest and tell the president what he ought to hear has been squeezed out of the inner circle." His name was Mansour Hassan.

She said, "Please, talk to the president. Tell him frankly, candidly, what you think. We were in America," she was saying, "We came back very heartbroken, and he came back very disappointed in nearly everybody." She mentioned a number of actors in whom he was disappointed, including President Ronald Reagan, Prime Minister Menachem Begin, and others.

Mrs. Sadat and I walked together to the president. She cleared her throat and said, "Mr. President, Dr. Saad Eddin Ibrahim is here." The president looked at me and shouted, "I know you hate us! I know you hate us! I know you hate us!" I was mesmerized. I was frozen in my place.

What do you say to the president of your country, when he shouts at your face and says, "I know you hate us!" three times? I did not know what to do, but Mrs. Sadat said very quickly and very diplomatically, "Mr. President, Dr. Ibrahim is our guest. At least ask him to sit down."

He said, "All right. Sit down. Sit down," but in a very disagreeable tone. I sat down, and when I got up my strength and my courage, I said, "Mr. President, why this very warm reception?" He said, "What warm reception? Are you kidding with your president?" I said, "No, no, Mr. President. I'm sorry. Why was this reception not friendly, not warm?"

He said, "Because I know. Our daughter Dina," who turned out to be his daughter-in-law, actually, "told me that you hate us. You bad mouth us in your lectures and in your classes." I said, "Mr. President, I don't recall having a 'Dina' in any of my classes."

He said, "No, no. She was not in your class, but she heard from her friends." I said, "Mr. President, this is *'an'ana*—hearsay. Dina heard from her friends that I have said this and this, and you hear from Dina. Mr. President, is this the way decisions are made in Egypt?"

He said, "*Ikhras!* Shut up!" Again, another shouting match. He said, "No, that is not the way decisions are made. I just wanted to let you know how I learned about it." I said, "Mr. President, I am sorry. If this is the way you are going to evaluate things, I do not know why you are asking me to come here." He said, "I asked you to come here to tell me about the nonsense you have been writing and publishing abroad." I said, "Mr. President, what kind of nonsense? I publish a lot of nonsense." He said, "Are you kidding with your president again?" Every time I tried to be light, or I tried to be friendly, or I tried to be forceful, nothing worked. He was always bombarding me.

We had three hours of debate. He would ask me questions, or Mrs. Sadat would ask me questions. I would answer; I would give the best of my opinions. He got angry at me several times during those three hours.

Then, at 3 o'clock, he got up. He was in his shorts and a summer shirt. He said, "This is the time for me to do my exercises. I do not eat lunch, but I want you to have lunch with Jihan." I said, "Thank you, Mr. President." He apologized for having been angry at me, and he disappeared against the Mediterranean horizon.

That was the last time I saw the president. I tried to decline the lunch, to leave. I thought it might be a mere courtesy. Mrs. Sadat said, "No, we do not break presidential orders here. He said that you have to have lunch with me. We will have lunch together. It is a simple lunch." I said, "Well, it is late, and I still have to drive." She said, "No, it is not late. The sun does not set until 8 o'clock in the summer. We will have a quick lunch, and then you can be on your way." We had lunch, and she again apologized several times for the outbursts of President Sadat. She said, "Believe me, if your messages were not getting through to him, the meeting would not have lasted for three hours."

One of the things President Sadat had said was, "I don't know why you and the other Arab intellectuals are against me, against my peace initiative, and against the peace treaty. I would like to challenge you and all the Arab intellectuals to a debate. It can be at any place in the Arab world, in Egypt, or in the world at large. Could you arrange to have the leading Arab intellectuals for a debate?"

During our lunch, Mrs. Sadat said, "What about the presidential suggestion that you convene a meeting of Arab intellectuals, so the president can come and talk to you?" I responded, "Are you sure that he was really serious?" "Oh, yes, he was dead serious about it. He is coming to a dead end with so many of the Egyptian intellectuals, and he sees that the Egyptian intellectuals take their cues from other intellectuals in the Arab world. Therefore, he would like to have all of them, or at least a sample of them, meet and have a free debate. They will either convince him that he is wrong, or he will convince them that he is right, or they will reach a third formula that he can pursue accordingly." She gave me her direct telephone numbers so I could stay in touch with her on the matter.

I said, "Well, I am going to a conference in Rhodes tomorrow." She asked me to initiate a conversation with whomever was there among the Arab intellectuals and see if a conference with Sadat could be arranged. She actually started talking to me about the logistical details of when and how to arrange such a conference, and if Arab intellectuals would come from the United States, then it would be better to have the conference around Thanksgiving or around Christmas time, and so on.

I initiated conversations with some of the leading Arab intellectuals of that time who attended the Rhodes conference. There was a tentative agreement that they would consider attending such a meeting with Sadat. Yet, by the third or the fourth day, news began to arrive from Egypt that was very disturbing. Sadat lashed out at everybody in his famous speech of September 5. He arrested about 1,800 of Egypt's political actors, including all the leading intellectuals who happened to be in the country and had been publicly critical of his policies.

The Arab intellectuals who were in that Rhodes conference said, "How could you ever even suggest an idea of Arab intellectuals meeting with your president, when he is arresting all the intellectuals we know in Egypt?" I was, again, dumbfounded.

That was the way Sadat did things. He obviously had disregarded everything I told him. He listened to others, people whom Mrs. Sadat was afraid he would be listening to and who wanted to be hard-liners. He did it in one sweep, like he did with the Soviet expulsion, like he did with the centers of power. He arrested everybody from the far left to the far right, Islamists, secularists, Wafdists, Nasserists, leftists, you name it. Everybody was arrested.

Time went by, and I still held to my belief that Sadat was misguided. I was still, at heart, a pan-Arabist, a pan-nationalist, a Nasserite, a leftist. I had written articles criticizing President Sadat and his policies: his open-door policy; his political liberalization, limited as it may have been; his regional policy of reconciliation and historic compromise with Israel; and his alignment with the West, especially the United States. I criticized each one of these policies.

But time passed, and I began to see how far ahead of his time Sadat was. He told me, "The Soviet Union is going to collapse, and it is going to collapse because of its internal bureaucracy." He was almost sure. And, of course, I took it lightly at the time.

He assured me that none of the rejectionist Arab leaders would fight Israel. He assured me that these leaders are more interested in staying in power than in fighting Israel. He said,

> Go around the world. We can win; we can lose—Israel can win; it can lose—but the conflict will never be resolved by force. Two, regardless of who is right and who is wrong, bygones are bygones. There are more and more Israelis who will appreciate the fact that we have to live together. There will be more and more Arabs—even if they are a minority today—who will appreciate the importance of a historic reconciliation.[1] Therefore, the better we do it, the better everybody will be. That is why I made the decision.

On one occasion in the conversation, he was telling me he would arrest some of the people who were in the opposition, including the Coptic pope, Shenouda. I said, "Mr. President, if you arrest or if you dismiss the pope, you know that this would be the first time ever, in fourteen centuries."

---

[1]   *Musalaha tarikhiyya*

He took a deep puff from his pipe, and he said, "Who could have thought that I would go to Israel?" I said, "Frankly, nobody." "Well, I did it, and therefore, I will dismiss the pope. Even if nobody has done it in fourteen centuries, I will do it, because the man deserves to be dismissed."

My rethinking of Sadat began with the Iraq–Iran War. Saddam Hussein declared war on Iran in the autumn of 1980. As the war dragged on, long after Sadat's assasination, the words of Sadat began to echo in my mind. Sadat said that other Arab leaders were interested in personal aggrandizement, not in solving the Arab–Israeli conflict, or liberating Palestine, or any such thing. When Iraq invaded Kuwait in August 1990, I became even more convinced of Sadat's vision of the region.

He understood the nature of the Arab despots. At the time I considered him an Arab despot himself, but he spoke about them as if they were really despotic and he was not. He felt that he was more democratic, more civil, and probably, in retrospect, he was. Despite everything that happened, by comparison, he was far more civilized than any of the Arab leaders then and since.

His words echoed. On the tenth anniversary of his assassination, I wrote a series of articles basically vindicating him and admitting my own shortcomings and mistakes in analysis. On the twentieth anniversary of his great trip to Jerusalem, we must remind ourselves that his vision for peace and reconciliation should not be in vain. The vision for which Yitzhak Rabin also worked should not be in vain. Because we in Egypt and in the Arab world all feel that many of the building blocks for peace that were crafted by Sadat, Begin, Rabin, Yasir

Arafat, Shimon Peres, and many others in the last twenty years, are now being systematically dismantled.

I am sorry to say that nowadays in Egypt, if one reads the Egyptian press, one will see a very quick sliding to what things were before Sadat's visit to Jerusalem. Mistrust is building up very quickly and replacing the trust that was very slowly and very painfully growing. This is something against which we have to guard. If we want to be true to the memory of Sadat and to the memory of Rabin, two great men in our region, we have to work again to put the vision for peace, for historic compromise, and historic reconciliation into effect.

Shibley Telhami

If I had to name the two most striking aspects of Anwar Sadat's legacy, they would be his understanding of the psychology of politics and of the power of leadership. As a student of politics, they strike me most and puzzle me most. In 1977, students of negotiations viewed Sadat's visit to Jerusalem and his declaration, "We accept to live with you in peace," as being rather foolish. It represented a major unilateral concession. In explaining his resignation as Egypt's foreign minister, Ismail Fahmy wrote that he told Sadat, "If we take the plane and go to Jerusalem, the act implies the automatic recognition of Israel and the termination of the state of belligerency. We play our two major cards and gain nothing. The gain is all on Israel's side and their bargaining power is doubled." [1]

Sadat understood what many students of politics have come to understand since. The game is much more dynamic than they previously appreciated. Once one side makes a large unilateral concession of this sort, the polity of the other state forces that state to redefine its interests and to see its interests differently. The meanings of concessions change afterwards.

If one looks at what transpired in the negotiations, one would be hard pressed to see at what point the apparent concession that Sadat made in his speech in Jerusalem affected anything that happened in the Camp David negotiations. Still, one can see many benefits deriving from that concession.

---

[1]   Fahmy, *Negotiating for Peace in the Middle East,* p. 257.

I say this because this debate is still being waged today, in various capitals in the Arab world, as well as in Israel. Should Israel move ahead and say, in principle, "We agree to a Palestinian state before territorial agreements are made, before concessions are extracted on Jerusalem," or should such a concession come at the end of the negotiations? I am not suggesting that this debate has been settled. Rather, there is something profound here that Sadat understood, that many students of politics did not understand. The game of politics is always a dynamic between domestic politics and foreign policy and, clearly, the impact of dramatic foreign policy gestures on domestic politics is profound.

The second point is that Sadat highlighted to me, as a scholar, the power of leadership. In some ways, I was humbled by what Sadat did. I did not predict the 1973 war, and I certainly did not predict that Sadat was going to go to Jerusalem. In fact, I challenge anyone to produce someone who did predict that those two things were going to happen. Scholars did not know that such moves were possible. We did not even contemplate the possibility of these moves taking place when they did. Good scholars have to look back, not at what is wrong with the leaders, but what is wrong with themselves, in not having any inkling of what the political leadership would do.

It is a profound insight that change in history usually occurs because of bold leadership. Had Sadat listened to Ibrahim Kamel or anybody else in the Foreign Ministry or Egyptian politics more broadly, there is no way that he would have done what he did. He would have gotten the same advice given in newspaper pages and in scholars' academic books. A leader cannot be limited to what his advisers have to say, because, in fact, bold acts of leadership change the world, they change people's perceptions of the world, and they enlarge the realm of the possible.

It is not a coincidence that if one surveyed public opinion in Egypt or elsewhere, one would have found no support for an agreement of this sort. But the minute Sadat flew to Jerusalem, the world was different, and everybody's perceptions were different. If one surveyed Egyptian opinion again, right after the fact, the results would have been different.

Although Sadat's personal style played a large role in Egypt's foreign policy, it is no less important that he conducted his policy in a world that differed markedly from that of his predecessor. Whereas Sadat and Gamal Abdel Nasser were different kinds of individuals, perhaps even more significant was the fact that Egypt after 1967 was not the same Egypt as the one of the period before the war. Certainly, the 1967 defeat and the rise of oil states, which limited Egypt's influence in the Arab world in the 1970s, had much to do with Sadat's focus on Egypt. Although Sadat may have affected the shift on the margins, the trend toward the entrenchment of statism in the region was already underway.

This is not to say that Arabism lost its meaning in the Arab world. It had not in Sadat's era, and it has not now. Sadat viewed Egypt's interests as coming first, but he certainly saw Egypt as the leader of the Arab world. He wanted to revive the leadership role that Egypt had in the Arab world, and he thought it was a historic and inevitable role.

Sadat's view is still important, because what I see happening in Arab politics today is the rise of a "new Arabism" that is being portrayed as a type of neo-Nasserism. In fact, it is acquiring some Nasserist symbols, and Nasser himself is being revived in some of the literature. There is a movie about Nasser that is popular.[2] There is a lot of coverage of Nasser. There is some revival, not just in Egypt, but in the rest of the Arab world, of Nasser.

But, in fact, if one looks closely at this new Arabist movement, it is not a Nasserist movement. It is a Sadatist movement wearing a Nasser garment. By this I mean that none of the Arab elites who are advocating this believes that there will be a single, united, Arab state. Everyone within this movement does believe that Arab states have much in common, and if they join in coalitions and collaborate on some of the common issues, they can do much more than they can alone.

This process taking place is completely outside the control of states. By contrast, the Nasserism of the 1960s was state-led. Today's Arabism is being driven by markets, the new media, and technology. New kinds of media have arisen in the region, some of it broadcasting from London, Rome, or the capitals of the Middle East. These media are mostly market-driven. They are trying to cater to the broadest Arab population, because the owners of the media outlets want to maximize their audience, primarily for profit but also for influence. In so doing, the Arabic language is emerging as a factor that defines the size of the market. One does not want to sell just to Egypt, but also to Syria, Saudi Arabia, and Morocco. As a consequence, the media are catering to the market and creating products that the market wants: shows that land-based national televisions stations are not providing. At the same time, on the political level the new media focus on issues that unify Arabs, not divide

---

[2]   *Nasser '56.*

them, and avoid domestic issues so as not to be left out of certain markets.

As a consequence, the new media highlight issues of foreign policy and regional unity, thereby creating a new unity of ideas among certain elites, across the board, in the Arab world. This movement is sometimes mis-characterized as a pan-Arabist movement. I do not see it that way. It is hard to know where such a movement is headed. It is hard to know how it is going to be captured, and eventually by whom. But I think it is a phenomenon that is there and that is going to be a factor in Arab politics, including Egyptian politics. No one can ignore it: not Egyptian president Husni Mubarak, not Jordan's King Hussein.

Let me end with the vindication of Sadat's legacy. I certainly think, eventually, Sadat will be fully vindicated in most of the Arab world. Saad Eddin Ibrahim wrote his paper for the Washington Institute in October 1993.[3] It was not a coincidence it was just a month after the Oslo Accords were signed, and it reflected the hope that flowed out of Oslo.

The suggestion I am making is that there is a clear connection, in Arab debates about Sadat's legacy, between how Sadat is read in the Arab world and how the peace process is going. If one looks at the debates about Sadat today, in 1997, they are not the same debates that took place in October 1993. Scholars must keep that in mind as well.

---

[3] Saad Eddin Ibrahim, *The Vindication of Sadat in the Arab World*, (Washington D.C.: Washington Institute for Near East Policy, 1993).

Discussion

Ahmed Maher el-Sayed, Ambassador of Egypt: I have two quick observations. First, the quotations that Ambassador Shamir read appear to accredit the idea that a leader need not listen to the advice of experts. This is a dangerous idea.

With regard to Dr. Ibrahim's remarks about how he saw the press in Egypt sliding to a pre-November 1977 sort of attitude, this seems to be a symptom. He did not not explain why this is happening, and this seems to me to be a serious lacuna.

Shamir: I was trying to explain the way Sadat thought about these issues, and how his decision-making process materialized. I think that those quotations faithfully reflect Anwar Sadat's approach. I expressed no opinion as to whether it was a good approach or a bad one.

As a former ambassador, I certainly would advocate that decision makers take more advice from their diplomats and other functionaries. I wish that the present prime minister had listened more to certain advice that was given to him. Each decision maker has his own style, and I was speaking about the style of Sadat.

Ibrahim: I did not go into the reasons why the Egyptian media, and the Arab media in general, is sliding to a pre-1977 mode of portraying Israel as the enemy. It is disturbing, and I am disturbed by it.

I know the reasons. One of the reasons is Israeli prime minister Binyamin Netanyahu, who is perceived, rightly or wrongly, accurately or inaccurately, as a very arrogant, provocative person who is humiliating not only the Palestinians but the Arab world. The sense of respect and dignity that the Arabs expect, even when they are weak, is very important. If the Israeli leadership does not recognize this, then the region will slide back, and that is a cause for concern.

If people are to be true to the legacy not only of Sadat but also of Yitzhak Rabin, they must stem that slide at its cause. Here, the role of the United States is very important, although I do not want to dwell on that.

Question: *None of the speakers have really addressed the issue of Sadat's possible economic motivations for his diplomacy. The bread riots of January 18 and 19, 1977, constituted one of Sadat's most embarrassing and difficult moments in power. Yet, Sadat long maintained that there was no real economic motivation or rationale for his trip to Jerusalem. What do those who have studied the situation more closely feel about an economic motivation.*

Ibrahim: I would not dismiss that as a factor. Whereas Sadat had his own grand design for peace and for the region, certain events probably affected the timing of his efforts, and one of them was the food riots of January 1977. The confrontation with the Islamists in July 1977 was another element.

In our conversation, Sadat told me that there are two sets of forces in the Middle East. One is the set that wants to maintain conflict, sometimes under the rubric of pan-Arabism, and sometimes under Islam. Then there are the forces of peace. Every time the forces of peace hesitate, they are allowing the extremists to occupy center stage.

I think that is what has been happening nowadays. When the moderates and the pro-peace forces hesitate or drag their feet, then they are allowing the likes of Islamic Jihad and Yigal Amir to ascend. The former killed President Sadat and the latter killed Prime Minister Rabin. Both claimed that God was speaking to them directly and ordering them to do what they did. If forces of that kind grow, then the agenda-setting will not be done by rational people, but by the most fanatical elements in the region.

Robert Satloff, The Washington Institute: *Would any of you care to comment on Sadat's evolution from being a Muslim Brother in his early days to being a foe of the Islamists at the end of his days? What went wrong?*

Ibrahim: One thing that President Sadat never realized is that the Muslim Brothers whom he knew were different from the Muslim Brothers he released from jail in 1971. What he did in 1971 was to negotiate with the elders of the Muslim Brothers, people from his age cohort. What he did not realize was that the Muslim Brothers had gone through a very deep split in the late 1960s, in prison. They had asked themselves the question, "Why have the Egyptian people not supported us when we are so pious and so good?" There were two answers, one by Sayid Qutb, and one by Hassan Hudaybi. Qutb's answer was that the Egyptian people, like their leadership, are bad, and they all ought to be brought down, whereas Hudaybi said, "We overplayed our cards. We used violence in a country that doesn't like violence, and that is why the Egyptian people did not rally to our support."

It was this second camp with which Sadat negotiated. But many of the younger ones who were released at the same time were followers of Qutb. They believed that the state is repugnant and the society is repugnant; these are the members of Islamic Jihad. It was this younger group that ultimately killed him.

Shamir: We spoke about many issues in which Sadat turned out to have impressive foresight, but he also made mistakes. One of his mistakes was that he did not read correctly the challenges to his authority in domestic politics. At the beginning, he thought that it was leftist groups that presented the greatest challenge. To counterbalance the left, he encouraged the Islamist movement. As Professor Ibrahim has suggested, he was working on the false assumption that they were the same Islamic activists with whom he had associated before—the Muslim Brotherhood. He did not realize the ideological change that had taken place in this movement when, under the guidance of Sayid Qutb, the thrust of *jihad* turned from a struggle against the outside world—Western imperialism—to inside Egyptian society, challenging the legitimacy of the Egyptian state itself. When he realized that, it was already too late. Radical Islam had been unleashed and it brought about his assasination.

Question: *On the point raised by Shibley, on the new media in the Middle East: Isn't Egypt losing the war for control of the new media in the Middle East, simply because the new media are now controlled by the Gulf states? Aren't the non-state-sponsored, Gulf-owned media outlets far more popular than the government-managed Egyptian media?*

Telhami: This is an interesting question, but I do not think the question is Egypt versus the new Arab media. I think it is states versus the new Arab media. Egypt, in a way, lost the media war by the 1970s anyway. Among the vehicles of leadership that Egypt had in the 1950s and early 1960s were the media, which Egypt mostly dominated. Egyptian media were influential all over.

As a way of protecting themselves, most Middle Eastern states emphasized their own media. Egypt's role in the media declined by virtue of the need of other states in the region to protect themselves against transnationalism. So one can say that while transnational movements were taking place all over the world, from the 1950s through the 1970s in the Middle East, there was a trend of entrenchment of state institutions, including information agencies. What appears to be happening now is that the Middle East is catching up with globalization in the information arena.

It is not so much that some of these media are controlled by Gulf businessmen. It is that the logic of the media is very different from projecting the point of view of a given state in the region. The new media are being driven by the market. They want to cater to the broadest market, and they are driven by the economics of information. As a consequence, states are losing control.

This media are listened to. They are creating new identities that are different, especially among elites, because, as was pointed out, most elites in the Arab world will read *al-Hayat* even before they read the local newspapers. They will watch Dubai television or MBC (a London-based satellite station) before they will watch a local television station.

The new media are creating a new identity, and it is consequential not only in the sense that every government must take it into account when it is acting, but also in terms of broader issues like normalization of relations with Israel. Even as governments have signed treaties with Israel, businessmen have said, "If you go to Israel, then you are not a member of our board, or our club, or our union."

five

Egypt, the Peace Process, and Egyptian–Israeli Relations, 1977–1997

Abdel Monem Said

Ehud Ya'ari

Samuel Lewis

Sadat's trip to Jerusalem made peace possible, but that peace has not always been as warm as the parties would have liked. The director of the influential al-Ahram Center for Political and Strategic Studies, Abdel Monem Said, expresses Egyptian frustrations with the outcome of the peace process that Sadat began, and respected Israeli journalist and Middle East expert Ehud Ya'ari outlines an Israeli view. Samuel Lewis, who served as the American ambassador in Israel while many of the details of this peace were being worked out, gives his own assessment of the challenges of making peace between Arabs and Israelis.

Abdel Monem Said

I have been expecting somebody to ask the question, if Anwar Sadat were alive today, how would he behave? What would he have done? What would he think of the situation? Of course, one might argue that if Sadat were alive, the Middle East might be facing a very different situation. One can, however, draw from Sadat's behavior at least three major lessons of paramount importance to our discussion of today's situation.

First, Sadat understood how to define his goals and stick to them. In reading about Sadat, I am always reminded of a book I once read about why the white settlers defeated the American Indians. There are a hundred reasons why the Indians lost, among them technological inferiority and internal division. One reason especially struck me. If the native Americans took siege of a European fort, and in the middle of the siege a herd of buffalo passed by, the native Americans would run after the buffalo. They abandoned their goal. Sadat never did that.

Therein lay Sadat's problem with his bureaucracy. Bureaucracies want a multiplicity of goals. They want to keep the Arabs happy, they want to keep the nonaligned happy, they want to keep the Africans happy, and they want to keep the Islamic world happy. Sadat's gaze remained fixed on his final goals. His primary goal was restoring Egyptian territories, and his secondary goal was peace.

The second lesson that can be drawn from Sadat's thinking is his understanding of the contradiction inherent in negotiations. In any negotiation, each party wants to maximize its interests, while each party also wants to reach an agreement. These two interests cannot always be reconciled. Sadat understood this contradiction very well. He knew when to press and when to make concessions, and he never lost sight of the final goal of reaching an agreement. He did one thing that I think is not very fashionable in the art of negotiation. Many people enter negotiations with a high price and work their way down. Sadat worked on changing the environment of negotiations, thus making the Israelis and Americans change their priorities. To have Egypt as an ally for the United States and as a peaceful partner for Israel became higher priorities than winning far-reaching Israeli concessions.

Third, Sadat understood global conditions. He knew that the West would triumph in the Cold War, and he acted as such. He had a vision of how to reintegrate Egypt into the Western world. Leaders in the region face quite a different challenge today, since the world has moved from being bipolar to being multipolar. Choices about allegiances are much harder to make than they were in Sadat's day.

With these lessons in mind, I would like to discuss the peace process that Sadat began. Egyptian–Israeli relations went through two stages after his death. After the Camp David Accords, momentum diminished. Discussions about autonomy failed to produce results, and the Israeli government went on a settlement-building spree. The Lebanon War in 1982 and the *intifada* beginning in 1987 hampered progress further. In fact, the entire decade of the 1980s was lost to the peace process.

In the 1990s, Egyptian–Israeli relations warmed because of the progress of the peace process. There were Madrid and Oslo, and Egyptian–Israeli trade grew from about $10 million of non-oil products in 1991 to about

$80 million in 1996. Egyptians used to visit Israel only in tens or in hundreds. In 1996, about 30,000 Egyptians visited Israel. In 1996, 326,000 Israelis visited Egypt, and more than half of them went beyond the Sinai Peninsula to visit the Nile Valley. A process was underway. Now, however, in 1997, the process is not only stalled, it is collapsing.

I see six fundamental deficits in this process of normalizing relations. First, a gradual process allows those who oppose the process on historical or religious grounds to sabotage it at very little cost. In addition, at least part of the current Israeli government, if not all of it, is against Oslo. Prime Minister Binyamin Netanyahu will say, "I'm with Oslo," but he never forgoes a chance to say it was a disaster for the Israeli people.

The second major deficit is the loss of a frame of reference. Since the inception of the peace process, everybody has talked of land for peace. But gradually all of the occupied territories became disputed areas. The Egyptian experience was full withdrawal for full peace. People are talking in a much more incremental way now.

The third deficit is the imbalance of power. This makes at least some Israelis, particularly those in power, feel that they can get away with things because of that. Even more important, external powers believe that such an imbalance is proper.

The fourth deficit is that only a few of the current leaders in the region understand geoeconomics, but all are obsessed with geopolitics. Shimon Peres originated the idea of a "New Middle East,"and he was ridiculed in the Arab world and in Israel. His conception of a common market, trade, communications, and the like was considered idealistic. In fact, it is the only realistic option, if this peace is to happen.

Number five is that the human aspects of this process have been downplayed. People in this process have been considered to be wholly economic animals; once they get their dividends or they get their money, they will be happy for peace. Jews and Arabs are much more complex than that. They have come with their own cultural and historical baggage, and there is nothing in the peace process that can deal with it. The Jews have a history of persecution and sacrifice. There is a persistent theme in Jewish history of being oppressed by numerically superior foes. This is not a negotiating ploy; it is a real historical and emotional complex. To many, the Arabs are merely the most recent in a long line of opponents.

Ironically enough, it is the reverse for the Arabs. Arab history contains many instances of how a few soldiers from outside powers can control their lives. How many British soldiers occupied Egypt for 70 years? How many Ottoman soldiers occupied the Arab lands for 400 years? Arab history is mostly the story of small minorities using technological prowess, skill, and deceit to control Arabs' lives for centuries. Israelis, who are numerically weak, technologically advanced, and very highly connected with the West, remind Arabs of this recurrent feature of their history.

Finally, the peace process became hostage to the United States. The United States has election cycles, it has Congress, it has a strong Jewish community, and it depends on the determination of a president. President Jimmy Carter was willing to devote time to Arab–Israeli peace, and he got results. So did President George Bush. But Ronald Reagan was not willing to devote the time, nor, probably, is President Bill Clinton. Negotiations depend on the American factor, and if there is no American factor, there are few alternatives.

Taking all that into account, what would Sadat have done today? Everyone knows the current state of affairs, and everyone knows it is not working. Sadat would have had to think of something. I came up with five crazy ideas.

First, Sadat might have thought of an international conference in Jerusalem. Following the explosion of a terrorist bomb in Israel, Mubarak convened an anti-terrorism summit at Sharm al-Shaykh with only a week's notice. Fourteen Arab states participated, and thirty heads of state attended. Why not convene a similarly dramatic and widely attended conference, and do it in Ramallah or Jerusalem?

Second, he might call upon the five permanent members of the Security Council to come together and impose peace. If the stakes were very high, if war were possible, and if violence and terrorism were ongoing, such a move might gain acceptance.

A third possible alternative might be to call on the United States to engage in multilateral negotiations similar to the Dayton talks held to make peace in the former Yugoslavia.

A fourth might be another trip to Jerusalem. He would have to think of something new to do on that trip, because he already got the magic from it before.

Fifth might be a regional conference, at least for the countries that sponsor peace—countries like Egypt, Jordan, the Palestinians, Israel, and Morocco. When one recalls that Egypt, Morocco and Saudi Arabia—all backers of the peace process—are not going to Doha, that means that something serious is going on.

Ultimately, however, peace has to be made between the peoples of the region. As a group, we Arabs and Israelis are worse off than we should be. We cannot point to the economic successes we should rightly have, because this conflict has been diverting us for decades. We must put this conflict behind us, not only for ourselves, but for our children. Leaders like Sadat can point the way, but in the final analysis we, the Arabs and Israelis, must make peace ourselves.

Ehud Ya'ari

W ere I to characterize the peace between Israel and Egypt, I would note that when my friend, Abdel Monem, goes to Israel, there is an uproar in the Egyptian press. When I go to Cairo Airport, I am still detained for two hours until the computer informs all the different agencies of my arrival. This gives some sense of how things are.

I have always believed that probably the best register of the twenty-year track record of the Israeli–Egyptian relationship can be reconstructed through the jokes, especially in Egypt, that accompany the peace process. One joke, which illustrates the mood of the late 1970s, concerns Prime Minister Menachem Begin's visit to President Anwar Sadat on Elephantine Island in Aswan. The joke went that Begin fell into the water. Sadat, the perfect gentleman, jumped into the water to rescue him, dragged him to land, and gave him mouth-to-mouth resuscitation. As the two men stood dripping on the shore, Begin said, "Thank you, Mr. President, you've saved my life." And Sadat said, "Please don't tell anybody about this incident. Our people should be convinced that the two of us can walk on water."

There are no longer leaders in either country who try to convey this impression to their peoples. In many ways, peace between Israel and Egypt, stable and somewhat stagnant, is a virtual peace. It is stable, it is ongoing, yet it is loaded with adversity, with suspicion, with confrontational tones. The conflict is resolved between the two countries, but the spirit of the conflict persists.

Peace is there, and it is not there. The most illustrative issue, from the Israeli viewpoint, would be why Israelis prefer to go for the fifth and sixth and seventh time to vacation at the casinos of southern Turkey and not to the casinos of Cairo. Every summer, middle- and lower middle-class Israelis make a vote of confidence in Turkey and express their doubts about Egypt.

The other day, I was looking at a paper that I wrote ten years ago for The Washington Institute, entitled "Peace by Piece," which tried to assess the first decade of peace. There would be very little I would have to change today. That is not a good sign.

I hereby would like to offer some brief reflections on the situation. A cold peace between Israel and Egypt sometimes deteriorates into a sort of cold war. In both cases, neither side shoots, but the quality of the relationship, the atmosphere, and the sentiments are changing too often. Along the way there have been important periods when it warmed up, but this is not one of these periods. Things are happening today in Egypt that I would not have believed could happen. When a rumor spread in Cairo recently that a certain Lebanese singer, Jihan Murad, was of Jewish origin, an instruction was issued to Egyptian broadcasting and television not to play her records. This ban was lifted only when a letter arrived from the Lebanese ambassador confirming that she came from pure Arab stock.

In the worst days of the conflict under Nasser, the Jewish singer Leila Murad was popular on Egyptian radio. Today, something has happened. I am not speaking about such anecdotes as the publicity given to a lawsuit demanding that Israel return the 300 pounds of gold that was taken from Egypt to build the golden calf during the Exodus, spoken about in the Bible. Yet, this is also part of the atmosphere.

The second point has to do with the domestic scene in Egypt. Number one, President Husni Mubarak has decided, for reasons relating to the domestic situation in Egypt, to realign the regime with what I would call its "neo-Nasserite" elements, heavily represented in the Egyptian Foreign Ministry, to be able to confront better the internal fundamentalist challenge. The regime cannot repay the left in domestic currency: The president will not abandon his free-market economic policies, as some people on the neo-Nasserite left would like. But he can repay them for their domestic support through foreign policy. This is the origin of the occasional strain between the United States and Egypt, not only with regard to Egyptian attendance at the Doha Conference but also in regard to some of the policies Egypt pursues vis-à-vis Israel.

The final point has to do with the collapse of the notion of the welfare state in Egypt following the peace treaty with Israel. This collapse was not a result of the peace treaty with Israel, but it was concurrent with it and it placed an enormous strain on the Egyptian bureaucracy, the intelligentsia, and the middle class at large. This strain is reflected in the suspicious attitude these groups tend to adopt vis-à-vis the advantages of peace with Israel.

Israel in recent years had a coalition under Labor, which I describe as a coalition of practical Zionists, such as the Labor Party itself; anti-Zionists, such as the Arab members of the Knesset, whose votes were crucial; and post-Zionists, such as Yossi Beilin and Yossi Sarid. That was one coalition, and its agenda was regional. For this coalition, the relationship with Egypt was fundamental.

The next coalition that came into being in Israel was a coalition between ultra-Zionists, such as the settlers' lobby; non-Zionists, such as the orthodox; and new Zionists, or the Russian immigrants, who are playing such an important role in the present coalition. For this new coalition, the domestic scene and the West Bank are the paramount interests. This negatively affects the Israeli government's attitude toward its partners in Egypt.

The widening circle of peace in the region, as slow as it is, has cast some doubts as to Egypt's centrality to the peace process. Much of the blame goes to the various Israeli governments that have been in power. I think that the late Yitzhak Rabin, certainly Shimon Peres, and absolutely Binyamin Netanyahu, were trying to bypass Egypt. They sought to play their cards with the Palestinians and the Jordanians without Egyptian participation. Prime Minister Rabin and King Hussein made an enormous effort to ensure that the Egyptians were nearly the last to know about the Declaration of Principles that was signed in Washington in 1994. Egypt played a role, leading to Oslo and afterward, that is underappreciated. Not only was the Camp David formula the frame of reference for Abu Mazen throughout, but the Egyptian role was much more active than is widely understood. Indeed, the whole idea of Oslo emerged from a meeting in Ismailia between Prime Minister Rabin and President Husni Mubarak, in which Mubarak sold Rabin an idea given to him by Peres. That idea was "Gaza first" and came to be "Gaza–Jericho first." Once the Oslo Accords were signed, there was an attempt, also in the Labor Party, to restrict Egypt's involvement in the process.

The view from Egypt was that the Israelis were making headway in the Gulf and North Africa. Under the terms of Shimon Peres's notion of a new Middle East, Israel was trying to design for itself a leadership role in the region independent of whatever partnership it might have with Egypt. Then Israel started to hear voices in Egypt arguing against normalization of relations. That was a very important point, because thereafter Egypt abdicated its role as the leader pushing everybody else forward and became the advocate of slowing down normalization.

On the one hand, President Mubarak used the issue of nonproliferation to stall and suspend the multilateral track. On the other, he cast himself as the only Arab leader upon whom Yasir Arafat could depend. For the Egyptians, the formation of this so called "Gaza–Cairo axis" allowed them to regain some leadership of Arab solidarity and a degree of coordination on the peace track with Israel that did not exist before.

Three things are important to keep in mind. One, no deal with the Palestinians is possible without the active support and blessing of Egypt, for a very simple reason: Whatever the final status deal may be, it will entail concessions from the Palestinian Authority. It is my opinion, so far confirmed by every Jordanian with whom I have spoken, that Jordan cannot and would not take upon itself to be the Arab sponsor of any concessions offered by the Palestinian Authority. Therefore, Egypt's role is crucial, inevitable, and should be welcome.

Two, the performance of the Israeli–Egyptian peace should not be allowed to slide further down a slippery slope. A minimal degree of cordiality, restraint, and exchanges is absolutely indispensable. Certainly, more effort can be invested in trying to remove the stumbling block that the Nuclear Non-Proliferation Treaty poses to multilateral negotiations. Yet, this issue is more of an excuse than a real disagreement, and some of the language used in Barcelona on the nuclear issue can be adopted or readjusted to create some formula acceptable to both Egypt and Israel.

My last point concerns Israel. I believe that Israel, at some point, will return to the realization that Egypt is and will remain the key to the peace process. As President Sadat used to say so often in his last years, there is no war and no peace in the Middle East without Egypt.

Samuel Lewis

Abdel Monem Said's analysis of what is needed to regain momentum in the peace process has a certain amount of validity, but it is also rather ahistoric. I have been teaching a course this semester on the history of the Arab–Israeli conflict. In preparing my lessons, I have been very much struck by the fact that ever since 1967, which is really when the peace process started, there have been periods of considerable success and long periods of considerable stalemate and/or failure. The United States has been associated quite prominently with the periods of success. The United States also has been around during the periods of failure, and during those periods of failure Washington has taken initiatives to get the process restarted, like the Rogers plan and the Reagan plan.

I defy anyone to find a period of great success in the peace process in which the real impetus for the progress did not start in the region. The progress has come when the situation, to use a now overly familiar term, has "ripened" in the region, and when the right leaders were in place to take advantage of the ripeness. At that point, it has indeed taken the U.S. role to make the process move successfully. They could not do it alone, but the United States cannot do it alone, either. That is where I disagree with Abdel Monem's emphasis on the U.S. "absence" as a major factor in the current stalemate. The United States is not absent. The United States is very much involved and has been involved continuously since the Madrid Conference of 1991.

The second point that Abdel Monem made with which I would take issue is the idea that the focus of the peace process has been lost. As Abdel Monem described it, Sadat defined the equation as a complete peace in return for all of the territory, and somehow the process is now confused. In fact, UN Security Council Resolution 242 did not promise complete withdrawal. The entire debate between June and November 1967 over 242 was a debate in which some parties tried to make 242 require a complete Israeli withdrawal, leaving no margin for negotiation over territory. That debate ended with 242 not requiring a withdrawal without negotiations.

But more fundamentally, his point appears to confuse the Egyptian–Israeli conflict, which historically lacks genuine conflict over the two countries' interests, with the much more complicated Palestinian–Israeli joint claim to the same land. It is not the same thing, and it has never been. It is extraordinary that, objectively, Egypt and Israel have no reason ever to have gone to war with each other. Egypt got into the conflict because of the Palestinian problem. Anwar Sadat made peace while sticking to his primary goal, which was to get all of the Sinai back. Making peace was subordinate to winning the return of the Sinai.

Sadat did not have as a primary goal ensuring that the Palestinians would get all of Palestine. Sadat had a political problem: He could not be seen in the Arab world as betraying the Palestinian cause. In the event, he got as much as he could for the Palestinians at that time. Under the rubric of Camp David, he gave them the ability to pursue their own peace efforts. Sadat made peace, however, not for the Palestinians but for Sinai and for Egypt.

To say that the peace process cannot be put back on track unless it gets back to the pure definition of full withdrawal from the territory is to turn history on its head. Doing so confuses the Egyptian–Israeli peace with a different kind of dispute that ultimately can be settled only with some kind of territorial compromise. That is the direction that the Palestinian–Israeli negotiations have gone since the Palestine National Council, meeting in Algiers in 1988, adopted its declaration of independence and, by implication, Security Council Resolution 242. Yasir Arafat was then led, with great difficulty, to accept 242 formally in Geneva the next month.

Ehud's analysis was quite interesting. I especially liked his emphasis on the interaction of the two domestic scenes. It may well be that the crisis of success is at the core of the problem here. Madrid marked the first acceptance of a readiness for compromise that became clear only in the later Oslo agreement. When the Palestinians agreed to go to Madrid as part of the Jordanian delegation, that symbolized a change from "all or nothing" to "we will make our state on whatever land we can get." By the time they reached that conclusion, a succession of Likud governments dedicated to increased settlement activity, plus a new wave of immigration from Russia, had combined to make it far more difficult to figure out how to carry out a Camp David–kind of compromise than it would have been in 1979.

One of the great tragedies of history is that the Palestinians were not prepared to come to the table for the autonomy negotiations in 1979 following the Camp David guidelines. Egypt tried its best to represent Palestinian interests, but it was really not possible for Sadat's representatives to make compromises and commitments on behalf of the absent Palestinians. Those negotiations failed for many other reasons, too, but I think that was the fundamental one. It was a miscalculation on Sadat's part to believe that he could represent the Palestinian interests when Egypt knew relatively little about the situation on the ground and, more important, when Egypt was unable to concede anything on behalf of the Palestinians for fear of being seen as traitors.

There is another challenging element at work here. For years, the Israelis had said, "You just get us together, face-to-face, with the Egyptians and with the other Arabs, and let us negotiate face-to-face." Sadat got himself together face-to-face with the Israelis. There was a brief moment between his visit to Jerusalem and the Ismailia conference on Christmas 1977 which was bilateralism writ large. It was a moment when the Egyptians and the Israelis had a chance to make peace without the Americans.

The failure of the Ismailia conference was a milestone. From that moment on, Sadat gave up on bilateralism, turned back to President Jimmy Carter, and put his stock in the United States to produce for him what he could not extract alone from Menachem Begin.

What I take from that history is that there is something very strange about the problem of negotiations between Israelis and Arabs. It is not a lack of communication. It is a lack of knowledge and understanding of each other. One of the extraordinary things about the Camp David negotiations was how much Israeli intelligence knew about Egypt as a country, yet how little Israeli leaders knew about Egyptians as a people. When the Israelis finally met their Egyptian counterparts in the course of negotiations, they found they were talking past each other 95 percent of the time.

We in the U.S. government watched this happen. Our role in the peace process, especially in the early years, was to try to interpret the Egyptian meaning of

Egyptian words to Israelis, and the Israeli meaning of Israeli words to Egyptians. We translated their ideas. It is not an easy role, and Americans are not very good at it sometimes, but we were there, and we did our best. That was a big part of our job.

Egyptians, for example, have a historical view of their own place in the region. I did not find that Israelis understood that at all, and I do not think they understand it today. It is not that they have not read excellent books, but somehow it has not sunk in that Egypt is a very special thing in the region, in Arab culture, and in the world. In fact, what may be the wisest book written to date on the subject of Egyptian–Israeli negotiations is one by Professor Raymond Cohen of Hebrew University named *Culture and Conflict in Egyptian–Israeli Relations: A Dialogue of the Deaf.*[1] He wrote a second volume when he was a fellow at the U.S. Institute of Peace, *Negotiating Across Cultures,* which deals with America's problems of cultural gaps in our negotiations with a number of countries around the world.[2]

Culture and Conflict deals with the Israeli–Egyptian cultural divide and how it has influenced the efforts to negotiate throughout the whole period of the peace process. There is an awful lot of brilliance in it. One of his premises is the one with which I started out: There is no objective reason whatsoever why Egypt and Israel should ever have been enemies, let alone have fought four or five wars. Yet that is what has happened. Cohen says the following:

> Through war and peace, fruitless contact and stumbling negotiation, a clear pattern emerges. It's

---

[1]   Bloomington: Indiana University Press, 1990.
[2]   Washington, D.C.: United States Institute of Peace, 1997.

summed up by the subtitle of this book: between
Israel and Egypt there was a dialogue of the deaf.
Separating the two sides were not irreconcilable
interests, megalomaniac ambitions, still less soaring
ideals, but a cultural chasm. Each side imprisoned
within the confines of its own habits, traditions,
language, and, most important, assumptions about the
way people think and behave, neither was able to
make itself understood to the other or make sense of
the other's equally futile attempts at communication.
Like tourists caught on different sides of the Niagara
Falls, Egyptians and Israelis could only mouth and
gesticulate at each other across the roaring, spray-
filled divide in grotesque and mutual incoherence.

Just why this incompatibility was such a prominent
factor in the negotiations and how it made itself felt
are the subjects of this book.[3]

There is more to learn from this book than anyone on
this panel can explain about why the Israeli–Egyptian
relationship, twenty years after peace, is sometimes
almost a cold war, and certainly a cold peace.

A few examples from history will illustrate this
point. The Ismailia conference in December 1977 was a
crucial moment when bilateral negotiations failed.
Begin, a man of detail, legalisms, and certainly
determination, came to Ismailia with a detailed
Palestinian autonomy proposal. Sadat, a man of vision
with a broad goal and a set of clear priorities, came to
Ismailia wanting a vague declaration of principles
sufficient for him to absolve his responsibility to the
Palestinians. He wanted to move quickly to negotiations
about regaining his land.

---

[3]   *Culture and Conflict*, p. 7.

Begin and Sadat talked past each other. It got hot. No one would open the windows. They finally could agree only on a procedural step: They would convene two committees, the Jerusalem Political Committee and the Cairo Military Committee, to carry negotiations forward.

Begin emerged from Ismailia believing that the meetings were a great success, because he was a man of procedure. He had no comprehension of Sadat's cultural approach toward this conflict. He did not understand that Sadat needed something to protect his pride as an Arab leader protecting Palestinian interests, but he certainly did not want or need a detailed framework for a compromise that would produce less than full withdrawal and a Palestinian state.

Sadat emerged from the Ismailia meetings convinced that Begin was impossible, and that he could never work with him. In fact, he never really did work directly with Begin again, or try to, even at Camp David.

Another example is well known. In January 1978, at the first meeting of the Jerusalem Committee, Begin made what he never understood was an insulting public reference to the Egyptian foreign minister as a "young man." He did not understand why, in Arab culture, that is something of an insult. Sadat had probably already decided he was fed up with Begin anyway, but Begin's remark gave Sadat the excuse he needed to break off the negotiations, turn back to President Carter, and put his faith and proxy in Carter's hands.

A third example: In Arab culture generally, a grand gesture demands reciprocation. When I went once to Begin with one of 50,000 requests for a few voluntary "confidence-building" concessions to smooth the negotiating atmosphere with the Egyptians, he said, "Sam, nobody gets something for nothing."

I am afraid there still is much cultural incomprehension in this conflict. It does not mean the two countries cannot live in peace. They have no real reason not to live in peace. It does mean it is going to be tough, slow sledding to make it into a warm peace.

Discussion

Ahmed Maher el-Sayed, Ambassador of Egypt: To be very brief, I will make my points in telegraphic form.

I did not think that this conference was intended to create what I would call a Sadatist fundamentalism. We have heard many times, "What would Anwar Sadat have done?" The question is not what Sadat would have done. Sadat has been dead for many years. Circumstances change, and people change. I think what we want in this conference is to see if we can preserve the spirit in which Sadat took his initiative.

With regard to my friend Ehud's presentation, I am repeatedly amazed that the Israelis always consider that whatever concerns they have are real. They are concerned about Iraqi chemical and biological weapons and about Iranian ballistic missiles. But when Egyptians are concerned about the nuclear capabilities of Israel, this becomes an excuse, a pretext, a manifestation of "neo-Nasserite tendencies." I do not understand. Why is it that the Israelis can have real concerns and Egyptians cannot?

The second point regards the story of "Nasserites." I would appreciate very much if Mr. Ya'ari could explain to me what "Nasserite tendencies" are and how this trade-off works between the internal and external policies of Egypt. I do not know who these "neo-Nasserites" are in the administration and in the Foreign Ministry, in particular. The story that Mr. Ya'ari tries to make up about Mubarak having to deal with the "Nasserites" is very strange.

The truth of the matter is that the Arab dimension of Egypt is a fact of life. History, geography, and culture indicate that part of the Egyptian personality is its Arab dimension. This is something the Israelis chose to forget at one time. They tried to take Egypt away from its Arab dimension. They thought that Sadat would acquiesce. In fact, he never did.

This brings me to a point that Ambassador Lewis made, that Sadat's aim was Sinai and peace. I agree with that. But peace means a comprehensive peace, the solution of the Palestinian problem and Israel's problems with the surrounding states. Anything less would not be a real peace. It would be a cold peace. The Middle East has seen such a peace, and there is violence everywhere.

One cannot have peace, which was one of Sadat's basic aims, unless it is a comprehensive peace. I heard Sadat himself say, "We will have a Palestinian state. I will have to liberate Sinai first, and then we will work for a Palestinian state and for the solution of the rest of the problems."

I do not think Egypt is looking for a role. I think it is the role that is looking for Egypt. Everybody has recognized the essential role of Egypt. Even if Egyptians did not want this role, this role would come to them because their indispensable contribution to the peace process is something recognizable.

Another of the Israeli dreams and fantasies is that Egypt's role is to deliver the Palestinians to the Israelis. Every time the Israelis want to impose something on the Palestinians, they come and say Egypt should convince the Palestinians to accept it. If Egypt does not, then there are murmurings in Israel, Washington, and many other places about how the Egyptians are not very helpful.

I do not want to get into the semantics of UN Security Council Resolution 242. Even if some people say that 242 does not call for total withdrawal, which is something that Egypt contests, it does not negate the fact that the territories are occupied territories. It is not a question of these territories being disputed territories. They are occupied territories. Whether Israel should withdraw from all of them or part of them is something that has been debated for many years. I think Sam Lewis has been confusing two things. It is not Abdel Monem who has been confusing the question of the territories and the illegality of occupation and the illegality of settlements.

With regard to the U.S. role, Egyptians think that it is indispensable. It is crucial, however, that the United States be a fair partner and not put pressure on only one side in the negotiations.

The last point regards the recall of the Egyptian delegation from Jerusalem in January 1978. I was part of that delegation, and Sadat did not recall us because of Menachem Begin's speech. The delegation was recalled because in meetings between Secretary of State Cyrus Vance and the Egyptians and the Israelis, everybody got entangled in legalistic discussions about texts and what not to do. Sadat thought that, in this legalistic discussion, his vision of peace between the Egyptians and the Israelis would be lost.

I would have many other points, but I have to let others speak, too.

Ya'ari: We are witnessing in Egypt a debate over foreign policy that is one of the liveliest in many years. In this debate neo-Nasserites are pitched against those who seek some adjustment and reformulation, in some way, of the Sadat legacy. The hearts of many Egyptians are still with Gamal Abdel Nasser, but their minds are already with Sadat. Dr. Saad Eddin Ibrahim has recounted his own transformation.

In Egypt today there is a foreign policy that plays to the hearts of many Egyptians, and it makes the foreign minister very successful on the domestic scene. I am not sure that the success on the foreign scene matches the success on the domestic scene. Recent Egyptian policy represents a very important departure from some of the golden rules of President Sadat, as described earlier in this conference.

Ambassador Maher, Israel is not asking and does not expect Egypt to deliver the Palestinians. Any compromise, any deal Israel will have to make with the Palestinians will also entail some concessions from the Palestinian side. It will be less than full withdrawal to the June 4, 1967, borders and will not include complete Palestinian control of East Jerusalem. We all know that. They will need a cover, and Egypt can give them the cover. What is really missing is an Israeli–Egyptian prior understanding regarding respective roles in the region. Such an understanding can be tacit, quiet, or even implicit. It may not sound very nice or polite, but Israel will need the Egyptians to accept and agree to the general contours of the arrangement in the Palestinian–Jordanian arena. I will put it very bluntly, because I am not representing anybody. Israel will have to remain a more senior player on the Palestinian scene once the final status deal is concluded—*in sha allah,* God willing—and Egypt will need to accept this fact from the outset.

Shimon Shamir, former Israeli ambassador to Egypt and Jordan: Let me try to take the discussion from the government-to-government level, discussed by Ehud Ya'ari and Ambassador Maher, to the people-to-people dimension, on which all three speakers made some important and thought-provoking points.

I would like to add one observation on this subject. The hate literature against Israel has increased since the beginning of the peace process. There is now an orchestrated campaign in Egypt against Israelis. Unfortunately, this campaign has been successful in realizing its objective, just as Yitzhak Rabin's assassin succeeded in accomplishing what he set out to do. The rejectionists in Egypt succeeded in effectively blocking the process of people-to-people dialogue that began to develop as a result of the political facts created by the two governments.

Because of this, the new Cairo Movement's courageous and principled support for dialogue is significant. Certain relations between Israelis and Egyptians exist in some areas. Businesspeople are working with each other, and the media people know each other quite well. Still, there is no genuine dialogue between the two societies. The Cairo group identified this problem accurately, and it is now engaged in an intensive campaign to get Egyptian support for this simple principle. They are telling the Egyptian public: Let us talk to the Israelis; let us know them better; we do not have to agree with everything they say, but without dialogue, the problems that this peace process is facing will continue.

Question: *Ambassador Lewis said at one point that the opportunities for progress start with the dynamics in the region. American initiatives like the Rogers plan, which were introduced when there were no positive dynamics in the region, have not worked. What has been said here should make people less optimistic, and perhaps even* *pessimistic, about the prospects for peace in the near future.*

What has been said, in particular with regard to Israel, concerns some very fundamental societal changes going on that have political repercussions for the composition of Israeli political power. There are also some similar kinds of changes occurring on the Arab side and in Egypt. That being the case, where is this dynamic in the region that is going to make it possible to get the process moving again, and how soon?

Lewis: I am in a very pessimistic frame of mind. I just came back from the region, and I do not see the constellation of leadership now that will provide a new spark for the United States, or anyone else, to blow into flame.

Israel is going through a series of crises internally. The prime minister is mistrusted by everybody in his own camp, as well as by all of the Arab leaders and some others in the world. Arafat is under great pressure from various forces in his camp. The Egyptians, like other Arabs, are going to be more preoccupied with the unfolding of the Iraq crisis than they are with the Palestinian issue for some time to come.

The next opportunity for a really successful American initiative may lie in the next crisis in the region, and I do not know that it is very far off.

Robert Satloff, The Washington Institute: *Before we end this panel, Abdel Monem, you have some comments you want to make?*

Said: First, Egypt established the Arab League under the monarchy in 1945 and entered the war with Israel in

1948. Egypt's involvement with the Palestinians predated Nasser, and it will continue after anybody related to him.

Second, the institutions of the Foreign Ministry and the Egyptian Army are nationalist institutions. In the Egyptian sense, that means that they represent what the country or the leadership of the country would like them to do. I can go on and give a lot of examples, but the theory that the Foreign Ministry somehow represents a "wing" of Egyptian policy is simply not true.

Third, I would like to touch briefly on the issue of the culture. When we started the dialogue in Copenhagen with our Israeli colleagues, one Arab said, "We want to reach a final solution to this problem." The words "final solution" for our Jewish–Israeli friends were historically loaded, but in Arabic have no such connotation. In another instance, the Israelis kept referring to "The Six Day War." One of us said, "Do you have to remind us every minute that you defeated us in six days?" We now refer to the wars by their dates—the June War, the October War, and so on.

At the same time, I must say that language is not a big issue in my experience. I encounter differences in Arabic when I talk with people from the Gulf or people from the Maghreb, and even in my own country between different classes and between urban and countryside.

Fourth, when I went to Tel Aviv and Jerusalem, I felt like I was in familiar cities. I knew them from television, from reading, and from talking. It was very dramatic for me to visit Damascus or Doha, because I did not know much about them. When I went to Beirut and Tel Aviv, I felt that I knew them very well. I see them a lot on television.

We see Israeli television, all of it, every day. By the way, it is a bit of a disappointment for some Egyptians who thought that Israeli television would be much more entertaining than Egyptian fare. It is not. The Israelis are very serious, debating and fighting all the time. Israeli television is a bit boring, but interesting. It can be seen in Cairo, and everybody can get it. I think Israelis are getting most of our television, too. But we both watch CNN.

Fifth, the peace process has often been linked to the U.S. role. I think that is very valuable, but what if the United States becomes preoccupied with other domestic or foreign issues? It creates a vacuum and allows the anti-peace forces to jump in. I value the American role; however, what happens if the United States is not very determined? There are variations from one administration to another.

On the issue of withdrawal, I concur with Ambassador Ahmed Maher. The United States continued to say that settlements are illegal until 1980 or 1981. Since then, Washington has said in the letters for the Madrid conference and others that the United States has not changed its position.

six

Egypt and America: Looking Backward, Looking Forward

Peter Rodman
Robert Pelletreau
Robert Satloff

As important as Anwar Sadat was to the cause of Arab–Israeli peace, he was perhaps even more important to the global interests of the United States. Yet, the promise of the U.S.–Egyptian relationship has occasionally led to some disappointment. In this section, former Kissinger aide Peter Rodman assesses the "Gaullist" aspects of Egyptian foreign policy; Robert Pelletreau, the former U.S. ambassador in Cairo as well as assistant secretary of state, examines the fundamental importance of the bilateral relationship; and Washington Institute Executive Director Robert Satloff looks to the future of U.S.–Egyptian relations.

Peter Rodman

In strategic terms, the significance of Anwar Sadat lay in his reversal of alliances. Each of the presentations here has talked about the Egyptian–Israeli relationship, but in the geopolitical context Sadat's significance lay in his rejection of the Soviet embrace and his throwing himself into the arms of the Americans. This was a repudiation of the foreign policy that Gamal Abdel Nasser had conducted since 1955. What Sadat did by this reversal of alliances was to weaken the Soviet-backed radicals in the region and to tilt the balance of forces in the Arab world more in favor of the pro-Western moderates.

This was the decisive event in the history of modern Middle East diplomacy. It was the turning point that changed the structure of the Middle East. From that moment in July 1972 when Sadat expelled Soviet troops and advisers from Egypt, he was relying on the United States. It was just a little bit before that event that he opened up a backchannel contact with the White House. Sadat was convinced that the United States "held all the cards."

We all know that the modern peace process began under U.S. auspices a little while later, after the October War, with the Egyptian–Israeli and Syrian–Israeli disengagement agreements in 1974 and the Sinai II agreement in 1975. When the Suez Canal was reopened in 1975, the geopolitical context was certainly in Sadat's mind: He insisted that the first ship to come through the canal be a U.S. aircraft carrier.

There was no doubt in Sadat's mind about what he was doing in this wider geopolitical context. The essence

of his geopolitical vision was his alignment with the
United States. He saw the United States as the country
that could help Egypt achieve its objectives. He aligned
himself against the Soviet Union and all the radical
forces in the region that the Soviet Union had been
helping to sustain, principally Syria.

I saw even Sadat's visit to Jerusalem in 1977 as a
reflection of this, and to my mind Martin Indyk's 1984
study is the best analysis of that decision.[1] One of
Sadat's most important motivations in going to
Jerusalem was his dismay at a particular trend in U.S.
diplomacy. In pursuing a "comprehensive" solution, the
Carter administration brought the Soviet Union and its
Syrian clients back into the game. It did so without any
apparent strategy to neutralize Syria and other radicals,
whose main goal in life was to prevent Sadat from
ending his state of war with Israel. The Jerusalem trip
was Sadat's way of forcing the game back into the
bilateral Egyptian–Israeli framework, which of course
meant under American auspices. Even though he may
have disagreed with Washington's tactics at this point,
Sadat's basic strategy was to stay within the U.S.
framework, make peace with Israel, and stay out of the
trap of Soviet and Syrian obstruction.

Now, fast-forward twenty years to an Egyptian
foreign policy based on somewhat different strategic
perceptions. There was the remarkable spectacle of an
Egyptian foreign minister saying in an interview a year
ago that he regretted the collapse of the USSR because
of the resulting "lack of international balance."[2]

---

[1]   *To the Ends of the Earth: Sadat's Jerusalem Initiative*
(Cambridge, Mass.: Harvard Middle East Papers, 1984).

[2]   "Interview with Amr Moussa," *Middle East Quarterly*
(September 1996), p. 62.

Egypt has begun to see itself as a kind of counterweight to U.S. dominance in the Middle East and in the world at large, a counterweight to the U.S.–Israeli alliance. Egypt no longer sees itself as part of an American-led coalition of moderates resisting radical influences. Egypt's more nationalist foreign policy is not in and of itself a problem for the United States. But Egypt's foreign policy is at the very least more Gaullist, and that can be a problem for the United States.

There may be something inevitable about this pursuit of Gaullism. Something important has changed in the structure of international politics with the collapse of the Soviet Union. Many countries are realigning themselves as counterweights to America's so-called "hegemony." The Russians and Chinese are clearly playing this game, as are the French. The tectonic plates are shifting because there are many countries that think the world is a little too unipolar for their taste. They see "multipolarity," as something that needs to be restored to the international system.

If Egypt sees itself as playing a Gaullist role in this manner, some difficulties are bound to come up. If coalitions are being formed to impede the United States, Washington is bound to notice it sooner or later. For example:

• On extension of the Nuclear Non-Proliferation Treaty (NPT), Egypt made itself the obstacle to what was clearly a priority goal of the Clinton administration. The administration saw extention of the NPT as absolutely vital to counter the possibility that weapons of mass destruction would fall into the hands of those radicals that the United States considers to be the major threats in the world today.

• Egypt agitated against Turkish–Israeli military arrangements that the United States has viewed as quite consistent with its own strategic interest.

• Egypt has demonstrated an interest in bringing Syria back into the diplomatic family, whereas the U.S. strategy appears to be to keep Syria a little bit off balance as long as Syria remains a potentially disruptive element in regional diplomacy.

• Egypt has sometimes been out of step with the United States on policy toward Iraq.

• Egypt even agitated against the Saudi–Jordanian reconciliation a year and a half ago, although the United States has wanted to foster that reconciliation since the Gulf War.

These are strategic issues—issues of U.S. geopolitical interests and perceptions. I have not even referred to the peace process disputes with Israel, in which Egypt sometimes seems to be egging on the PLO rather than trying to moderate it. The issues I raise are global U.S. geopolitical concerns.

My Egyptian friends sometimes say, "There is a division of labor here. We have relations with Syria, and we have our own relations in the Arab world. Let us handle it this way. This is in the service of the common interest, and Egypt is serving the common cause by its own means and its own context." There is some wisdom in this, but there is also a risk in this game of distancing itself that Egypt might appear to be an obstacle to U.S. policy. It is not an accident that Jordan now seems to be the Arab country that shares American strategic perceptions more consistently than does Egypt.

This is obviously a change from what Anwar Sadat represented. It could be called "Nasserite," but I prefer to call it "Gaullist," because I think that is what it resembles. Whether it will serve Egypt's interest in the long run remains to be seen. Ultimately, Egyptians will have to choose their own foreign policy.

To me, the Middle East is still a region of many dangers, of many radical pressures and radical forces. In the end Egypt still ought to value its link with the United States.

Robert Pelletreau

In this period of discontent with some of Egypt's recent positions, such as the decision not to attend the Doha conference or its ready rejection of the use of force against Iraq, one can sometimes forget how far Egypt and the United States have traveled together since President Anwar Sadat's historic visit.

Peace between Egypt and Israel became a reality, and it remains the cornerstone of all that has happened since. This includes the treaty of peace between Jordan and Israel. It includes four Palestinian–Israeli agreements. It also includes the initiation of direct and productive negotiations between Syria and Israel at the Wye Plantation.

Much has been said about the importance of Egypt in the Palestinian–Israeli dimension, but one should not neglect Egypt's importance to the Syrian dimension as well. I recall when the Madrid Peace Conference was in its closing hours, the American delegation was trying very hard to persuade the Syrians to agree to have the first bilateral meeting there at Madrid. We were running into an absolute stonewall. At one point then–Secretary of State James Baker turned to me and he said, "Go find Amr Moussa. We are going to need Mubarak's help on this." I did manage to track down the Egyptian foreign minister, and we did reach President Husni Mubarak, and he did get on the phone with Syrian president Hafiz al-Asad, and Syria ultimately did agree to have the first meeting right there at Madrid to get those negotiations off to a good start.

Egypt has also been very important in the multilateral process and the process of confidence building between Arabs and Israelis more broadly. That process has now suffered a serious reversal, the extent of which is most clearly shown by the fact that eight Arab delegations were present at Yitzhak Rabin's funeral—more than will be present at Doha.

The Arab delegations are staying away from Doha because Israel has been invited, because the peace process is foundering, and because the fragile flower of mutual confidence is wilting. The metaphor that I sometimes like to use about the peace process now is that the boat is foundering and people are no longer pulling on the oars. They are bailing to keep the boat afloat. As a consequence, the boat is no longer moving forward the way it was.

As President Sadat made the peace, I believe President Mubarak has kept the peace. Within Egypt's internal leadership discussions, President Mubarak has acknowledged that the Egyptian–Israeli border is the most peaceful and the most stable of any of Egypt's borders today. President Mubarak made clear just three days ago, when he spoke of Egypt's decision not to go to Doha, that this did not mean a slackening of Egypt's support for peace.

Turning to the Gulf region, it is worthwhile recalling that after Iraq invaded Kuwait, it was Egypt's leadership that brought the majority of the Arab world into the international coalition. It was Egypt's leadership that allowed the United States to call it a truly international coalition, and it was Egypt's contribution of forces to the liberation of Kuwait that was second in size only to that of the United States.

I was recently told by a Gulf foreign minister that the United States needed to continue to support Egypt because for them in the Gulf, Egypt is the high dam.

Egypt for them represents the high dam of stability against fanaticism, against extremism, and against instability throughout the region.

In addition to the two very strong pillars of the peace process and Gulf stability, Egypt and the United States have cooperated in a number of international peacekeeping efforts, from Somalia to Cambodia to Bosnia and elsewhere. Egypt has a proud record of participation in international peacekeeping efforts.

These are not actions that Egypt has taken out of love for or subservience to the United States. Egypt has taken these actions because Egypt perceived them to be in its own interests, and those interests were perceived to be running parallel in many cases to U.S. interests, through a process of virtually constant consultation and coordination between the two leaderships.

At those times when the United States has neglected this process of consultation or tended to take Egypt for granted, or Egypt has done the same, strains have inevitably developed. Egyptians are proud of their accomplishments. They are proud of their 7,000-years-plus of history, and they are quick to take offense if others seem to be trying to dictate policies to them or fail to recognize the great civilization that they represent.

The U.S.–Egyptian relationship thus requires careful and constant attention and management on both sides. By and large the two countries have been successful in doing that. When one compares the period since Sadat's visit to Jerusalem with the roller coaster relationship that existed before that time, one will find there have been ups and downs, but they have been in a much narrower band than existed before.

Both Egypt and the United States are complicated societies with complicated decision-making processes. It requires a great deal of study and understanding to have a real feel for what is happening.

One of the things I used to do in Cairo over my morning coffee was to read the front page of *al-Ahram*. I would test myself to see how well I thought I understood what was being reported, and what was happening, and why. It was a real exercise in humility for me to perform this test. In addition, my political and economic sections in the embassy did not welcome this exercise much because it often led to my asking them a lot of very difficult questions.

Two internal developments in Egypt are worth my mentioning. The first is Egypt's economic reform program, which has recently been turning a corner in terms of national growth, job creation, and unleashing the power of the private sector after years and years of centralized state control. The process is only beginning, and it needs to be encouraged.

The second internal phenomenon is the Islamist movement and its terrorist fringe. The Islamist challenge has been a major preoccupation for the Egyptian government over the past five years, and a challenge that the government has gradually been mastering. This challenge is not subject to a quick fix. It requires daily attention and daily action, both operationally and in terms of planning.

I would suggest that now is not the time for the United States to reduce its important assistance programs for Egypt, just at the time when governmental programs are beginning to yield positive results. Continuation of these vital inputs in the coming period will serve U.S. interests as much as they will serve Egyptian ones. Egyptian economic health and Egyptian internal political stability are important to the United States.

Egypt and the United States will differ from time to time on issues and on approaches. It is only natural that they should do so since, as I mentioned, Egypt is following its own policies and interests just as the United States is following its own policies and interests. Our two countries should take care to handle those differences within the framework of the broad established common interest that they have, and not let them become exaggerated.

Occasionally each country will be obliged to move in a way that creates some real unhappiness in the other country. I think back a few years ago to when the United States was working flat out to secure the indefinite extension of the Nuclear Non-Proliferation Treaty. As the final vote neared, it was what one could call "come-to-Jesus" time, and I participated in drafting instructions to "lean on" Egypt. Of course the United States putting pressure on Egypt in this way caused unhappiness and some strain in the relationship. It was, however, a matter of great importance to the United States.

Likewise now there is considerable unhappiness in Washington about Egypt's decision not to go to Doha. It was not an easy decision for the Egyptian government to stay away from Doha, but I can say honestly that it is a decision very strongly supported by Egyptian public opinion, the Egyptian media, and the Egyptian intelligentsia. It would have been very difficult for President Mubarak to go against those forces. The United States, ultimately, must understand this reality.

When Egypt and the United States work together, we can be a powerful force for peace and stability in the world's most volatile region. When we fail to work together for one reason or another, we are inevitably both weaker for it.

Robert Satloff

This is the second time in 1997 that I am giving a talk on U.S.–Egyptian relations. The first time was before the House International Relations Committee in April. That talk produced a couple of headlines largely because I prepared my testimony in the expectation that the State Department would appear on a panel before mine. In the event, State Department officials did not appear, and consequently, those of us outside the government attracted more attention than usual.

I am not going to reread my testimony on U.S.–Egyptian relations, but I would like to underscore a few themes, because I still believe what I said seven months ago. First, the modern era of the U.S.–Egyptian relationship began in the Cold War. There are two strong themes that animated the genesis of U.S.–Egyptian relations two decades ago. One of them—Egypt's move toward peace—lives on, while the other—Egypt's turn to the West—has disappeared.

In retrospect, one tends to forget that Egypt's turn to the West was perhaps America's greatest victory in the Cold War. It changed everything. The U.S.–Egyptian relationship that emerged in the mid-1970s reflected that shift as much as it reflected the shift of Egypt's direction in peacemaking. The relationship that emerged carried with it high levels of bilateral assistance, a close military relationship, and wide-ranging strategic cooperation. Today, however, the relationship is missing one of its two premises. It lacks a strategic dimension.

Out of the 1970s relationship four elements emerged: the strategic alliance, the commitment to peace, economic assistance and the pursuit of reforms, and an incremental approach toward domestic liberalization. Almost everybody would agree that the United States did its fair share. Part of the brilliance of Anwar Sadat and Menachem Begin was that they knew to cut a deal with Washington when Washington was in a very generous mood. Their deal has been confirmed over much of the last twenty years at an annual cost of more than $5 billion worth of U.S. assistance to these two countries. It is difficult to imagine any international actor today doing anything that would convince both ends of Pennsylvania Avenue that it is worth that sort of U.S. assistance. They both got a pretty good deal.

Economically, assistance to Egypt partially offset the loss of Arab aid. It helped build an infrastructure for the Egyptian economy. Recently it has given Egypt a vital cushion as it undergoes economic reforms. At the core of the U.S. aid effort is the belief that U.S. interests are served by a strong Egypt.

Over the past few years there have been a number of public disputes in the bilateral relationship. I will not list them, but I will note a couple of ironies. It is an irony that when the United States took military action against Iraq in 1996, it was President Husni Mubarak himself, not his foreign minister, who termed it a violation of international law. It is an irony that, within hours of the passage of this year's foreign aid bill reconfirming the $2.15 billion in U.S. assistance to Egypt, the Egyptians made the decision not to attend the MENA summit in Doha. Egyptians must comprehend that this sort of imagery has ramifications in Washington. One cannot avoid the fact that people in Washington, and certainly those in Congress, will see the timing as a slap in the face.

There has also been a certain vagueness as to where Egypt's relationship with Israel fits into Egypt's relationship with the United States. The relationship is both bilateral (U.S.–Egypt) and trilateral (U.S.–Egypt–Israel). Neither Washington nor Cairo has quite figured out which geometric formation, the straight line or the triangle, governs the relationship.

I remember very well when a senior Egyptian official came to this Institute and said privately to me and Martin Indyk (before he left the Institute in 1993 to enter the U.S. government), "Egypt, Israel, and America, working together: This is the triangle that counts." Since that time, the Egyptians have sometimes acted as though the peace process and Egypt's relationship with Israel would have no ramifications on the bilateral relationship between Washington and Egypt.

Here, the Egyptians have had a basic decision to make ever since Sadat died. They had a choice either to broaden peace to include other Arab parties or to deepen peace with Israel and hold up that peace as a model for other Arab parties. They chose to broaden peace, to seek others to join the circle. With the convening of the Madrid conference, that policy was validated. Peace was broadened.

Then the Egyptians faced another decision. The decision was whether to enter into a partnership with the Israelis or to serve as the peaceful competitor to the Israelis. They chose the latter, to compete rather than to cooperate. This was all done in the context of peace. No one should suggest that the basic elements of this peace are under threat, or that the Egyptian leadership doubts this. Maintaining the treaty is clearly in Egypt's national interest. Still, one would be remiss in not recognizing the drift that is now under way.

Having in such a brief and cursory fashion sketched
some of the problems facing the U.S.–Egyptian relationship, let me suggest a few policy recommendations. This
is done in the framework of recognizing that a relationship born in the 1970s lacks a 1990s core. I think we can
inject into this relationship a 1990s core relevant to the
current situation which would be to the benefit of both
parties.

I would suggest three elements: political, strategic,
and economic.

First, there needs to be far better dialogue on all
levels of government, institutionalized, regularized, and
formalized over time. These must include more than
political talks at the foreign ministry level and logistics
talks between the defense ministries. Washington and
Cairo need serious high-level strategic talks on a regular
basis. The partnership between Mubarak and Vice
President Al Gore is an important step in the right
direction but it is not, by itself, the answer.

Two areas ripe for strategic discussion are clear.
First, the peace process: As one looks toward 1999, final
status negotiations will likely result in a contractual
arrangement among two parties, Israel and the
Palestinians. In reality, this arrangement will be among
three parties: Israel, the Palestinians, and Jordan. But
there will be an overarching political arrangement
among four parties: Israel, the Palestinians, Jordan, and
Egypt. It is vitally important for the Americans and for
the Israelis to talk first with the Egyptians and the
Jordanians as a prelude to the real final status
negotiations with the Palestinians. If those negotiations
are to happen any time in the foreseeable future, as the
prime minister of Israel would like, then those informal
discussions need to take place now.

Second, the Gulf: Washington needs to talk at a very high and urgent level with the Egyptians about the future of the Persian Gulf. If there is "no war without Egypt and no peace without Egypt," then there is no great success for the United States in the Gulf without an understanding with Egypt as well. Washington does not need constant Egyptian participation in its activities, but it does need the absence of Egyptian opposition to American efforts. That can come only from serious and high-level dialogue.

I would like to make two specific suggestions regarding the U.S.–Egyptian economic relationship. I have made them before, and I believe they deserve further attention. First, I would like to change the mix. Every Egyptian businessman with whom I talk would agree to reduced dollar assistance if it were translated into increased Egyptian access to U.S. markets. If the United States took $100 million off the Egyptian aid program and increased access for Egyptian goods in America by an equal amount, almost everybody would happy.

Second, every Egyptian I speak to complains about the USAID bureaucracy in Cairo. Whether accurate or not, the perception is that the U.S. bureaucracy is sopping up a lot of the assistance money to Egypt. I support an increase in the direct transfer of assistance to the Egyptians, without any U.S. bureaucracy, but such a move would be far more likely to win congressional approval if there were less money in the overall pie. If one reduced the overall package by $50 million or $100 million and gave an equal amount directly to the Egyptians, most Egyptians would prefer that as well.

These moves would also be affected by a perception that aid to Egypt is linked to aid to Israel, but that is a topic for another discussion. In general, I think the operative principle should be that Washington not be kept hide-bound to old equations, because times and circumstances have changed.

Discussion

Pelletreau: Just two weeks ago I was in Cairo, and I spent some time with President Husni Mubarak. We talked about Egyptian attendance at Doha at some length. I urged him very strongly to find a way to go, and I suggested a way to go and not go at the same time. The Egyptians are not bad at doing that when they want to.

There was no question in my mind that he was very attuned to what he was hearing from all the elements of Egyptian society and what he was hearing from the broader circle of Egypt's international contacts. There were really no significant voices outside of the United States that were urging him to go to Doha.

It is perhaps a lesson to the United States that when the peace process falters, U.S. leadership across the board on all issues in the region is less solid. Every U.S. ambassador in the region knows that when the peace process is not actively moving forward with full U.S. engagement, it becomes harder to persuade others in the region to side with the United States, whether it is a question of Gulf security, nonproliferation, antiterrorism, or any of the other important issues that Washington has.

Abdel Monem Said, al-Ahram Center for Political and Strategic Studies: Divergences between Egyptian and U.S. policies have been exaggerated. The United States and Egypt share a strategic understanding about the Persian Gulf. This understanding may not be very elaborate nor might it cover every detail, but the United States and Egypt have agreed since the end of the Gulf War that the Iraqi leadership should not be toppled by military means. There is a shared understanding about the Arab–Israeli peace process as well, at least in general terms, despite the differences that sometimes arise. On some things, the Egyptian position is too close to the American position for American comfort. Egypt's position on the NPT was exactly the Bush initiative for arms control in the Middle East. The only difference was that Egypt took that initiative as a serious gesture to be implemented equally by all parties. American domestic politics played a role in shaping U.S. views on how that initiative should be implemented. On a host of other matters, ranging from bilateral trade to intelligence coordination to military coordination, cooperation is extensive.

On the issue of Doha, it was a very close call. There were many internal debates. Assistant Secretary of State Martin Indyk came to Cairo to make a special case for Egyptian participation. Yet, nobody argued that the Doha Conference would be beneficial. The argument for Egyptian attendance was merely that the United States wanted the conference to be held, despite the fact that nobody was preparing for it. Everybody knew that from a substantive point of view, the conference would be a failure. On the Israeli side, Prime Minister Binyamin Netanyahu has never shown any interest in this kind of normalization in the region. The issue was symbolic, to demonstrate that something from the peace process was still working.

Until three or four weeks ago, Egypt was inclined to participate in the conference at a low level. Egyptian attendance was to be symbolic, as a way to make the United States happy. Then three developments in the last few days came into the picture. First, Palestinian–Israeli negotiations and the accompanying American mediation bogged down. Second, there was American saber-rattling on Iraq. Third, Egyptian–Qatari relations flared up. These three factors tipped the balance.

Satloff: I would agree with you completely about the military-to-military relationship. I think two things are actually quite well understood on the two sides. One is the military-to-military relationship, and the other is the American deference to Egyptian needs on domestic stability. On these issues there is full agreement.

The issue with Doha is not just whether Mubarak sends a delegation. If one reads the transcript of Mubarak's press conference announcing the Egyptian government's decision not to participate, he was asked whether Egyptian businesspeople are going to Doha. To me, the position of a president should be that Egyptian businesspeople are free to do whatever they care to do. Mubarak went on to say that a few of them may go, but it would be a very small group. His message was that not only at the official level, but also at the business-to-business level, Doha is something in which Egyptians are not participating.

Samuel Lewis, The Washington Institute: Regarding Doha, it was very apparent to any close observer of the scene four-and-a-half to five months ago that Doha would be a flop if it occurred. The wisest course for the United States would have been to have sat down with the Egyptians at that time, and maybe also with the Saudis, and devised a way gracefully to defer Doha until the peace process was more promising. Such consultation would have avoided all of this "you are not a good ally" business that Washington has gotten into. I think it is ridiculous, and Washington failed by misreading the prospects for Doha months ago. The administration was just thinking that it could push Arab participation in Doha through on the strength of the alliance that has been described. I do not think that is the way to make an alliance work.

Secondly, why is it nobody says anything about the Saudis? The Saudis came out two or three months ago and said they were not going. Once they did that, Egypt was in a very difficult position. Nobody seems to care about the Saudi position or take it seriously. I think Washington missed the boat both ways: in ignoring the Saudi decision and not anticipating the Egyptian one.

Joseph Sisco, former under secretary of state: How does this all apply to the current crisis that the Middle East is in? President Mubarak has taken the view that he opposes taking military action against Saddam Hussein. Others in the Arab world have said so. Is there a way in which the United States can take military action and modify the position of Egypt and Saudi Arabia, or at least limit whatever the short-term damage might be from any use of U.S. military force?

The policy right now is on the right track. Washington is trying to exhaust all diplomatic remedies. I am extremely pessimistic that this will in any way result in a change in the position of Saddam Hussein. I am convinced that it is going to be necessary for the United States to use military force. If it comes to that point, that force should be in strength, and it must be sustained. One of the reasons for opposition to the use of military force in the area is that Washington lacks credibility. The last time it applied force it was a slap on the wrist, therefore leaving Saudi Arabia, Egypt, and the rest of the Arab world holding the bag.

Say President Clinton comes to the awful decision to attack Iraq. How can Washington begin to ameliorate the short-term damage that a U.S.-led strike on Iraq would do to U.S. influence in the region? First and foremost it has to do much more to get this peace process moving. Let me be very explicit. The administration disagrees strongly with the policy that Prime Minister Netanyahu has pursued since he came to power in Israel. I do not want to imply that there are not problems on the Palestinian side, but it is unacceptable from the point of view of the strategic interests of the United States for Israel to slow progress on the peace process. Washington has leverage to bring about some adjustment in the position of Israel and of the PA at this particular juncture. The United States can get a more serious dialogue.

I want to repeat that I am not placing the blame merely on Israel. Not at all. I agree with what Madeleine Albright said with respect to what Yasir Arafat needs to do and what Netanyahu's contribution has been to "create the environment that exists today." As an adjunct to the use of force, Washington has to be seen to be doing much more on the peace process, and here harnessing the help of Egypt.

Second, the United States flubbed in its whole CIA operation trying to create an opposition to Saddam Hussein. That process has to be restarted if it has not already been, because one of the reasons for opposition to the use of military force is that Washington does not have a political policy attached to that particular use of force. Therefore I suggest getting together with Egypt and Saudi Arabia and at least beginning to engage in terms of trying to develop a viable Iraqi opposition. I have been involved in a number of these operations, and frankly America is not very good at doing this kind of thing. Everyone knows this. Nevertheless, it would be very helpful to sit down with Mubarak and with the Saudi Arabians and say, "We cannot live with Saddam in the long run, you cannot, and yet you say to us 'Don't use military action.'" Unity is great, but not if it represents the lowest common denominator. It may very well be that the United States has to go it alone, but it must have its allies engaged.

Our Arab friends know that if the United States backs off, if it concedes, Saddam will be freer to develop his weapons of mass destruction. In the short and intermediate term, Saudi Arabia and Kuwait will be under threat. Such a situation harms Egypt's strong interest in Gulf stability, as well as America's own special relationship with Saudi Arabia.

What is needed here is an administration that has a strategy. Unfortunately, I do not see one.

Rodman: I agree with almost everything Joe said, with one or two caveats. It would be great in this context to have movement in the peace process to bolster America's position in the Arab world, but the administration has to be careful about that: Linkage is tricky. Last time, Saddam tried to use linkage to make himself the champion of the Palestinians. The danger is that if Bill Clinton seems to act under Saddam's pressure or blackmail, Saddam gets credit for whatever results. This does not help us, nor does it help the Egyptians or the Saudis.

I also want to make more explicit what is perhaps implicit in much of this discussion. The coming crisis may be the most important test of U.S.–Egyptian relations that Washington has faced in years. It is far more important than Doha. I am a little nervous that the

Egyptians might distance themselves from the United States, which would not be helpful.

The reality is that Egypt's interest with regard to Iraq is identical to America's, and all of our Arab friends have the same interest that we do, and the United Nations as a whole does. We have to prevail. If Saddam succeeds in what he is doing, if he is free to acquire weapons of mass destruction, he becomes the king of the Gulf. It will mean the reversal of the outcome of the Gulf War if Saddam gets his hands on a deliverable weapon of the kind that he wants to get. If the Egyptians are not with Washington this time, there will be a serious crisis in U.S.–Egyptian relations.

Satloff: *Could I ask our Egyptian guests to comment on the potential Egyptian position in the event the United States decides on the use of force against Iraq?*

Saad Eddin Ibrahim, Ibn Khaldoun Center: Let me start by noting that every time American speakers talked about a crisis this morning, I thought about the crisis in Arab–Israeli relations. If one were to ask all the Arabs here, to what does the word "crisis" refer, their unanimous answer would be the stalling and the undermining of the Arab–Israeli peace process.

I assure you that the sentiment in Cairo today, which was reported to me by my wife over the telephone very early this morning, was with regard to the funeral of Saad Wahba, a former president of the Egyptian Writers' Federation and a columnist for *al-Ahram*. It was a mass demonstration. Saad Wahba was a hardliner, and he is not known to many people here. He became a star with the Egyptian masses only in the last year and a half or two years, since Netanyahu came to power. He became the mirror image of Netanyahu in terms of being a hardliner. That is why I said yesterday that the Middle East is sliding steadily, and I am afraid swiftly, to a pre-1977 discourse. That is the danger.

I do not think that there is an Egyptian who will support military action in the Gulf against Saddam—not because of love for Saddam, but because of lack of American consistency and leadership in the region. The United States wants the Arabs to line up again in an alliance against Iraq. They want the Arabs to do it again when they hesitate even to say to Mr. Netanyahu, "Honor the agreements that were signed by Israel."

Satloff: *Could I ask the other Egyptian guests an even more pointed question? The American strategy is to exhaust diplomacy until the only option left is to move to military action. Should diplomacy be exhausted, would Egypt support military action?*

Muhammad Wahby, *al-Mussawar*: Diplomacy should not be exhausted only in the Iraqi direction. Diplomacy should be exhausted equally in terms of Mr. Netanyahu's stand. There is no diplomacy at all in this direction. Why should the United States be so active against Iraq and do nothing about Mr. Netanyahu? That's number one.

Number two, I found we were going in circles regarding U.S.–Egyptian relations. The substance of those relations is peace. No one can contest the fact that the substance is still there. What has happened? Egypt has some differences over this substance.

You mentioned a triangle of Egypt, Israel, and the United States. Who has defected from this triangle? Egypt? Not Egypt. Israel? Again, not Israel. It is Mr.

Netanyahu over the last two years. This group started talking about the crisis in the relationship between the United States and Egypt as if the whole strategic edifice that has been built over the last twenty years should collapse only because of a single dimension unrelated to the substance that you have identified: consensus on peace.

Peace is there. Everybody has agreed that Egypt is as committed as it has ever been. There are some differences, and the differences have arisen only since Mr. Netanyahu assumed power in Israel. Otherwise, I do not see any reason for a furor about a crisis in U.S.– Egyptian relations.

Samuel Lewis, The Washington Institute: Listening to this conversation reinforces a conviction that I have about the Iraq crisis. In 1991, major Arab states were afraid for their own interests after the invasion of Kuwait. In 1997, I do not have a sense that any of the Arab states feel their interests are involved at all. That is the big difference we have to face now.

seven

Sadat and the Pursuit
of Arab–Israeli Peace

Martin Indyk

Anwar Sadat will be remembered most for his decision to make peace with Israel and his accomplishment of that goal. Twenty years after his trip to Jerusalem, however, Egyptian–Israeli peace has not yet led to a comprehensive Arab–Israeli peace. One man actively engaged in the effort to construct a durable Arab–Israeli peace, Assistant Secretary of State for Near East Affairs Martin Indyk, reflects on Sadat and on the courage and vision he demonstrated leading Egypt toward peace.

Martin Indyk

I would like to discuss not one man, but two: not only Anwar Sadat, but also Yitzhak Rabin. As a policymaker and someone engaged in trying to make peace, it seems to me that these two great statesmen had much in common, and there is much to be learned from the role that they both played in the process of making peace in the Middle East.

Anwar Sadat was, perhaps, the originator of the peace process. With his historic visit to Jerusalem twenty years ago, he created a breakthrough that made everything else possible. Of course, that was not only because of the man himself, but because of the country that he led. Egypt is the strongest, largest, militarily most powerful, politically most influential Arab country. For it to make peace with Israel was something that made it possible for everything else to follow.

It is perhaps ironic that the twentieth anniversary of Sadat's historic visit to Jerusalem is within days of the second anniversary of Rabin's assassination. Both men broke the mold. The trip to Jerusalem and the handshake on the White House lawn with Yasir Arafat were dramatic events that changed the course of Middle Eastern history, and they were possible only because of these two leaders. Without them, there would have been no such events and, I dare say, therefore, no such breakthroughs to peace.

Sadat understood very well what he was doing. He always emphasized the psychological barriers to peacemaking and the need to break through them. Rabin very much followed his lead, for the handshake with Yasir Arafat was surely as important psychologically for ending the conflict with the Palestinians as Sadat's speech in the Knesset was to breaking the psychological conflict between Egyptians and Israelis.

Both men were leaders, in the sense that they understood the responsibility they had to lead their people: not to be led by their public opinions, not to be constrained by them, but rather, to get out ahead of them and to try to change the thinking of their publics. Of course, and perhaps not surprisingly, they both paid the ultimate price for doing so. Their lives were taken by assassins stuck in the old way of thinking and unable to accept the dramatic and determined effort that these two leaders were making to break the mold and thereby make peace.

Sadat and Rabin had much more in common. Both were strategic thinkers—they understood the strategic positions of their countries, the resources at their disposal, the balance of power in the region, and their ability to create change by understanding the relationship between force and diplomacy. For Sadat, this was most obvious in the way that he made war to make peace. The October War was a breathtaking example of the way in which Sadat, in his determination to make peace, understood that he had to shake up the status quo and give both Israel and the superpowers a reason and an incentive to change their attitudes.

In a different way, Rabin understood how the *intifada* had the potential to change the political relationship between Israel and the Palestinians. In the midst of the *intifada*, Rabin and I had a sumptuous meal at the Tel Aviv Hilton. Rabin smoked his cigarettes, ate, and delivered a lecture at the same time. He talked about how the *intifada* had created a new cadre of Palestinian insiders who took matters into their own hands, and how this would force a change in the political situation. At that time, he thought there was a potential to build an internal Palestinian leadership. In that sense, he was still stuck in the old mold of Israeli thinking. He quickly discovered the reality that there was no independent internal leadership, and that any decisions made by the Palestinian delegation to the Madrid Conference, were, in fact, referred to and made by Yasir Arafat.

In this particular instance, when Rabin realized that in fact there was no internal Palestinian leadership, he decided to deal with the Palestine Liberation Organization (PLO). This represented a radical departure in Israeli thinking, but Rabin was a realist—another quality he and Sadat shared. Rabin's decision to deal with the PLO came out of two realizations. First, there could be no peace for Israel as long as Israel was ruling over the Palestinians. The *intifada* brought that lesson home to him. Second, there could be no peace without the PLO. Post-*intifada* diplomacy brought that home to him.

I remember sitting with Rabin in March 1993, on his first visit to Washington during the Clinton administration. We were having breakfast. There was a conversation going on, and he gave his analysis pretty much as I am giving it to you. Ambassador Samuel Lewis said to him, "Well, if that's the case, why don't you deal with the PLO?" His answer was, "I can't meet their requirements. They want a Palestinian state with Jerusalem as its capital, and I can't meet that requirement."

Over the next six months, however, he came to the conclusion that while he could not meet their requirements, Arafat was prepared to meet Rabin's requirements. Those requirements were, at that time, Israeli control over security, no dealing with settlements until the final status negotiations, no dealing with Jerusalem until the final status negotiations, and Gaza first. When Arafat accepted those requirements in a letter in July of 1993, at that moment I believe Rabin decided to do the deal.

Why do I give these details when I am supposed to be talking about Sadat? Because at the time of the breakthrough with the Palestinians, there were those who said Rabin was pushed into this by Shimon Peres, or that Peres and Yossi Beilin had done this maneuver and basically presented him with a *fait accompli*, and Rabin accepted it.

At the time of Sadat's visit to Jerusalem and subsequently, there were those who said he did not really mean it when he made that speech in the Egyptian People's Assembly and said he was going to go to the Knesset. They said that he had not thought it through, but it was just like Sadat to do something dramatic like that. Of course, we know that he had carefully calculated the reasons why and the logical consequences for his actions, just as Rabin had.

It is critical to the peacemaking process to have leaders who are capable not just of reading the map, but of seeing the way things are connected to each other in realistic ways, so that they understand the logical consequences of their actions and others' actions. Only then can they move in a calculated way that can produce the kinds of dramatic results that they both did.

The importance of their relationship with the United States was a third thing that Sadat and Rabin had in common. Sadat, as we know, expelled the Russians to build a relationship with the United States. He said that Israel gets everything from the United States, from a loaf of bread to an F-15 plane; therefore, only the United

States can influence Israel. That is why he was determined to build a relationship with the United States. The United States was very slow to understand his purposes, and it took a war before Washington really paid attention to him. Then, in 1977, when the Carter administration tried to put together a Geneva conference on Middle East peace, I believe it inadvertently created the circumstances that led him to decide to go to Jerusalem. It is a long story, but the reality was that the Carter administration was pushing to get the Syrians and Egyptians and everybody else to Geneva for an international conference. For Sadat, such a conference was anathema, because that meant that his policy would be tied to Syrian policy. Further, he believed the Syrians would never go to Geneva, there would never be a conference, and he would not be able to make the peace that he was so keen on making. He took a shortcut to Jerusalem as a way of diverting Washington from its purposes and getting it to back his purposes.

Rabin also had a great appreciation for the role of the United States. In fact, in all of the obituaries and memorial speeches, it is often neglected just how much stock he placed on the strategic relationship that he did so much to help build between the United States and Israel. Maybe he learned something from Sadat, but he believed very strongly that the role of the United States was to support the process, not to lead the process. That was up to the parties themselves. He did not want the United States in the negotiations in the way that it is now. He wanted America to support them. He felt, from his perspective, that to have the United States engaged in the negotiations would inevitably make the United States the mediator between Israel and the Palestinians, or with whichever other Arabs they were negotiating. In such circumstances, Washington would have to move from a position of supporting Israel to becoming a mediator between the two parties. He did not want that.

Even though Sadat and Rabin appreciated the value of having a strong relationship with the United States, as well as the important role the United States could play in the peace process, both of them chose to act behind America's back. Sadat went to Jerusalem. He did not consult with us; he surprised us. Similarly, Rabin surprised us when he decided to do a deal with Yasir Arafat, which led to the Oslo Accords. It says something about those two men that they understood that, when it came to making peace, they had to deal directly with their adversaries: Peace is made with enemies, not with friends. They understood that peace is not made with the United States, but with their partners; and that the partnership is what matters. They understood the fact that both sides could gain, that it was a non-zero-sum game. They understood that to make the deal, one had to take account of the other side's concerns. Some of these concerns were psychological, in terms of insecurities, or for the Palestinians, in terms of recognition and dignity; others were tangible, in terms of territory. It was that understanding of the need to deal directly that was, I think, critical to their peacemaking capabilities, and which led to those two breakthroughs. They were also ready to take risks for peace. And that, I believe, derived from a combination of courage, vision, and a sense of urgency.

I conclude on, I am afraid, a fairly pessimistic note. It is difficult to be optimistic these days. I note for the record that it took some sixteen years from the time that Sadat went to Jerusalem—and the Egypt–Israel peace treaty was finalized a year later—to the time when there was another agreement struck on the White House lawn. I fear that it may take another sixteen years before another leader like Sadat or Rabin comes along with that same combination of courage, vision, willingness to take risks, and sense of urgency that combined to create the circumstances in which these two dramatic break-throughs—peace between Israel and Egypt and an agreement between Israel and the Palestinians—were possible.

I hope I am wrong. Certainly, the lessons that they hold out for peacemakers of the future should be clear by now. But what is also clear is that they both paid the ultimate price, and that it takes a special kind of courage to be a peacemaker in the Middle East.

Discussion

Question: *In a previous panel, Saad Eddin Ibrahim mentioned that he fears that there is a sense of a reversion to an almost pre-November 1977 atmosphere in terms of Egyptian views toward Israelis, and perhaps Israeli perceptions of Egyptians. Having just come back from Egypt, how would you evaluate Egyptian views about peace and what Egypt might be willing to risk for peace in the 1990s, based on the Sadat legacy about which you just spoke?*

Indyk: As I said at the beginning of my remarks, Egypt is the cornerstone of the peace process. The United States has learned through experience, good and bad, that if Egypt is involved in the process of negotiations, it becomes much easier to make progress. If Egypt is excluded, it becomes much more difficult. That is point number one.

Egypt, as a regional power, has its own calculations about its interests. They do not always coincide with America's own. Nevertheless, the U.S. relationship with Egypt is critical to Washington's ability to move the process forward. The Clinton administration will work with Egypt, despite the disappointments, because of the country's importance to the process and the administration's belief that the United States and Egypt share a fundamental commitment to peace and to the promotion of security and stability in the wider Middle East.

Now, twenty years after Sadat's trip, it is unfortunate that the relationship between Egypt and Israel has not burgeoned in the way that both sides had hoped it would. I am not going to go into all the reasons for that, but I want to give one example that I find particularly disturbing and that needs to be addressed urgently, by both sides.

Twenty years ago, the military on both sides led the way, whether it was the Kilometer 101 talks or Ezer Weizman's critical role in his relationship with Sadat. The military-to-military relationships were essential to the process of peacemaking.

Now, Egypt is reaching the end of a long process of force modernization and shifting its armed forces from dependence on Soviet equipment to the use of U.S. equipment. That means that the Egyptian army now is a formidable force, and it has been built up as a consequence of the peace treaty and the peace process.

The militaries on both sides are now barely engaging, except when it comes to the issue of arrangements in the Sinai. As a result, Israeli military planners looking at the Egyptian order of battle are now saying, "This is a real problem. There are real capabilities out there." Because there is almost no communication between the militaries, Israelis must infer Egyptian intentions. These assessments, which I believe to be overly pessimistic, can be tested only through a dialogue. That dialogue is not taking place, and it needs to take place. There is no reason why it should not take place. It is not a question of politics, and it is not a question of the peace process. It is a question of professional relationships that need to be built between the military on both sides.

After twenty years of peace, it should have happened already, and there is no reason why it should not happen now. If it does not happen it will negatively affect the overall relationship, precisely because the Egyptian military has strengthened and Israelis see that as threatening.

When I was the U.S. ambassador in Israel, I worked with Ned Walker—the U.S. ambassador in Egypt who is now about to be the ambassador in Israel—on this issue and on issues in the economic area, to try to build people-to-people relations between Egypt and Israel. Such relations are critical to the future of the peace treaty. Both sides need to take that seriously.

There was a time last year when the Egyptians made the calculation that they needed to build their relationship with the Israeli business community, because the business community was a force for peace. I think that was a correct assessment. But on both sides there is a kind of resistance that makes building such relationships very difficult. That is one of the reasons I very much regret the Egyptian decision not to go to Doha. The economic conference in Cairo last year was of great benefit to Egypt. The economic conference in Doha, which currently has 1,000 business participants registered, is a conference that will benefit the region, giving countries that lack vast oil reserves opportunities to showcase what they have to offer the international business community.

I fail to see why that could possibly be against Arab interests. The U.S. secretary of state and the secretary of commerce are determined to go, because the Clinton administration believes it is the right thing to do for the region and the right thing to do for peace.

Question: *Could you discuss the U.S. role? Does the United States have the courage that was there in Sadat's time and in Rabin's to help the parties make the leap that they need to do now?*

Indyk: Yes, the United States does have the courage. What I said about how Rabin and Sadat viewed the American role is important in this regard. Secretary of State Madeleine Albright has been saying for some time, "We cannot make the decisions for the parties. They are the ones who have to make those decisions. They are the ones who have to calculate what the risks and benefits are, and then decide to go forward." The United States can support them. The United States can urge them. The United States can underwrite them. The United States can do its best to reduce risks. The United States can give them its ideas, if they need ideas. In the end, however, they are the ones who are going to have to do it. That is certainly the message that she will be taking to them: "It is time, gentlemen, to move, and we want to see you move, and we are ready to support you in that process."

Supporting the process is something that the United States has been doing for the last four and a half years. When Rabin was moving forward and taking risks for peace, the United States had a very different role. It just had to get behind him and minimize those risks. Now the process is stalled and Prime Minister Binyamin Netanyahu feels that he has a different kind of mandate from the people of Israel. That mandate is to not take risks for peace, but rather to demand reciprocity and change the nature of the process. In those circumstances, Washington's role inevitably changes somewhat, but it is still very much a supportive one.

It is in that context of supporting the process that high-level U.S. representatives are going to Doha, because the conference is an institution of the peace process. Lack of U.S. support for that process and for those who decide to come in the face of opposition would send a signal that Washington is not prepared to stand by those who take risks for peace.

Question: *Clearly, Binyamin Netanyahu is no Yitzhak Rabin. At the same time, there are some important things about Netanyahu that need to be taken into account. He is, after all, leader of the Likud. Some of the things he has done are quite remarkable. First, he accepted Oslo despite the fact that he said he would not have signed it. It was significant that he got out of Hebron. It was quite amazing that he supported the further redeployment, despite the National Religious Party pushing him in the other direction. The "Alon-plus" plan, as a plan for the permanent hand-over of part of the West Bank despite all the problems that are involved, is significant as well. Perhaps sixteen years is a bit too pessimistic. Perhaps it is possible that, with all the setbacks and all the problems, the Israelis and the Arabs will reach an agreement sooner than sixteen years from now.*

Indyk: Absolutely. Sadat did not make peace by himself; he made peace with a Likud prime minister, Menachem Begin. In doing so, Menachem Begin was able to bring the people with him. Rabin had a one-seat majority, and it would have been extremely difficult for him to pull off a Hebron agreement had he lived. Netanyahu could do it. He has a significant margin of support for moving forward in the peace process. A Likud prime minister, without a doubt, could serve as a partner in the way that Menachem Begin did to Anwar Sadat. That is clear.

The problem is that Netanyahu finds himself constrained by his coalition. There is a gap between Force 17—the coalition partners who oppose territorial concessions and who threaten to bring his government down on any particular day—and the eighty-three votes for the Hebron agreement. His challenge is to break out of the constraints imposed by a minority and take advantage of the fact that a majority favors moving forward. That is a very difficult task, and I do not underestimate it for a moment, but I also believe it can be done.

Appendix A

President Anwar Sadat
Address to the Israeli Knesset
November 20, 1977

In the name of God, the Gracious and Merciful.

Mr. Speaker, Ladies and Gentlemen:

Peace and the mercy of God Almighty be upon you and may peace be for us all, God willing. Peace for us all on the Arab land, and in Israel as well, as in every part of this big world, which is so complexed by its sanguinary conflicts, disturbed by its sharp contradictions, menaced now and then by destructive wars launched by man to annihilate his fellow man. Finally, amidst the ruins of what man has built and the remains of the victims of Mankind, there emerges neither victor nor vanquished. The only vanquished remains man, God's most sublime creation, man whom God has created—as Ghandi the apostle of peace puts it: to forge ahead to mold the way of life and worship God Almighty.

I come to you today on solid ground, to shape a new life, to establish peace. We all, on this land, the land of God—we all, Muslims, Christians, and Jews—worship God and no one but God. God's teachings and commandments are love, sincerity, purity, and peace.

I do not blame all those who received my decision—when I announced it to the entire world before the Egyptian People's Assembly—with surprise and amazement. Some, gripped by the violent surprise, believed that my decision was no more than verbal juggling to cater to world public opinion. Others still interpreted it as political tactics to camouflage my intention of launching a new war. I would go as far as to tell you that one of my aides at the Presidential Office contacted me at a late hour following my return home from the People's Assembly and sounded worried as he asked me, "Mr. President, what would be our reaction if Israel should actually extend an invitation to you?" I replied calmly, "I will accept it immediately. I have declared that I will go to the end of the world; I will go to Israel, for I want to put before the People of Israel all the facts."

I can see the point of all those who were astounded by my decision or those who had any doubts as to the sincerity of the intentions behind the declaration of my decision. No one would have ever conceived that the president of the biggest Arab state, which bears the heaviest burden and the top responsibility pertaining to the cause of war and peace in the Middle East, could declare his readiness to go to the land of the adversary while we were still in a state of war. Rather, we all are still bearing the consequences of four fierce wars waged within thirty years. The families of the 1973 October War are still moaning under the cruel pains of widowhood and bereavement of sons, fathers, and brothers.

As I have already declared, I have not consulted, as far as this decision is concerned, with any of my colleagues and brothers, the Arab heads of state or the confrontation states. Those of them who contacted me, following the declaration of this decision, expressed their objection, because the feeling of utter suspicion and absolute lack of confidence between the Arab states and the Palestinian people on the one hand, and Israel on the other, still surges in us all. It is sufficient to say that many months in which peace could have been brought about had been wasted over differences and fruitless discussions on the procedure for the convocation of the Geneva Conference, all showing utter suspicion and absolute lack of confidence.

But, to be absolutely frank with you, I made this decision after long thinking, knowing that it constitutes a grave risk, for God Almighty has made it my fate to assume the responsibility on behalf of the Egyptian People and to share in the fate-determining responsibility of the Arab Nation and the Palestinian people. The main duty dictated by this responsibility is to exhaust all and every means in a bid to save my Egyptian Arab people and the entire Arab Nation the horrors of new, shocking and destructive wars, the dimensions of which are foreseen by none other than God himself.

After long thinking, I was convinced that the obligation of responsibility before God, and before the people, make it incumbent on me that I should go to the farthest corner of the world, even to Jerusalem, to address members of the Knesset, the representatives of the people of Israel, and acquaint them with all the facts surging in me. Then, I would leave you to decide for yourselves. Following this, may God Almighty determine our fate.

Ladies and gentlemen, there are moments in the lives of nations and peoples when it is incumbent on those known for their wisdom and clarity of vision to overlook the past, with all its complexities and weighing memories, in a bold drive toward new horizons. Those who, like us, are shouldering the same responsibility entrusted to us, are the first who should have the courage to make fate-determining decisions which are in consonance with the circumstances. We must all rise above all forms of fanaticism, self-deception, and obsolete theories of superiority. The most important thing is never to forget that infallibility is the prerogative of God alone.

If I said that I wanted to save all the Arab people the horrors of shocking and destructive wars, I most sincerely declare before you that I have the same feelings and bear the same responsibility toward all and every man on earth, and certainly toward the Israeli people.

Any life lost in war is a human life, irrespective of its being that of an Israeli or an Arab. A wife who becomes a widow is a human being entitled to a happy family life, whether she be an Arab or an Israeli. Innocent children who are deprived of the care and compassion of their parents are ours, be they living on Arab or Israeli land. They command our top responsibility to afford them a comfortable life today and tomorrow.

For the sake of them all, for the safeguard of the lives of all our sons and brothers, for affording our communities the opportunity to work for the progress and happiness of man and his right to a dignified life, for our responsibilities before the generations to come, for a smile on the face of every child born on our land—for all that, I have made my decision to come to you, despite all hazards, to deliver my address.

I have shouldered the prerequisites of the historical responsibility and, therefore, I declared—on February 4, 1971, to be precise—that I was willing to sign a peace agreement with Israel. This was the first declaration made by a responsible Arab official since the outbreak of the Arab–Israeli conflict.

Motivated by all these factors dictated by the responsibilities of leadership, I called, on October 16,

1973, before the Egyptian People's Assembly, for an international conference to establish permanent peace based on justice. I was not in the position of one who was pleading for peace or asking for a ceasefire.

Motivated by all these factors dictated by duties of history and leadership, we signed the first disengagement agreement, followed by the second disengagement agreement in Sinai. Then we proceeded trying both open and closed doors in a bid to find a certain path leading to a durable and just peace. We opened our hearts to the peoples of the entire world to make them understand our motivations and objectives, and to leave them actually convinced of the fact that we are advocates of justice and peacemakers.

Motivated by all these factors, I decided to come to you with an open mind and an open heart, and with a conscious determination, so that we might establish permanent peace based on justice.

It is so fated that my trip to you, the trip of peace, should coincide with the Islamic feast, the holy Feast of Courban Bairam, the Feast of Sacrifice when Abraham—peace be upon him—great-grandfather of the Arabs and Jews, submitted to God; I say when God Almighty ordered him, and to Him Abraham went, with dedicated sentiments, not out of weakness, but through a giant spiritual force and by a free will, to sacrifice his very own son, prompted by a firm and unshakable belief in ideals that lend life a profound significance.

This coincidence may carry a new meaning to us all, which may become a genuine aspiration heralding security and peace.

Ladies and gentlemen, let us be frank with each other, using straightforward words and a clear conception, with no ambiguity. Let us be frank with each other today while the entire world, both East and West, follows these unparalleled moments which could prove to be a radical turning point in the history of this part of the world, if not in the history of the world as a whole. Let us be frank with each other as we answer this important question: How can we achieve permanent peace based on justice?

I have come to you carrying my clear and frank answer to this big question, so that the people in Israel as well as the whole world might hear it, and so that all those whose devoted prayers ring in my ears, pleading to God Almighty that this historic meeting may eventually lead to the results aspired to by millions, might also hear it.

Before I proclaim my answer, I wish to assure you that, in my clear and frank answer, I am basing myself on a number of facts that no one can deny.

The first fact: No one can build his happiness at the expense of the misery of others.

The second fact: Never have I spoken nor will I ever speak in two languages. Never have I adopted nor will I adopt two policies. I never deal with anyone except in one language, one policy, and with one face.

The third fact: Direct confrontation and a straight line are the nearest and most successful methods to reach a clear objective.

The fourth fact: The call for a permanent and just peace based on respect for the United Nations resolutions has now become the call of the whole world. It has become a clear expression of the will of the international community, whether in official capitals, where policies are made and decisions taken, or at the level of world public opinion, which influences policymaking and decision taking.

The fifth fact, and this is probably the clearest and most prominent, is that the Arab nation, in its drive for permanent peace based on justice, does not proceed from a position of weakness or hesitation, but it has the potential of power and stability which tells of a sincere will for peace. The Arab-declared intention stems from an awareness prompted by a heritage of civilization that, to avoid an inevitable disaster that will befall us, you, and the entire world, there is no alternative to the establishment of permanent peace based on justice— peace that is not shaken by storms, swayed by suspicion, or jeopardized by ill intentions.

In the light of these facts which I meant to place before you the way I see them, I would also wish to warn you in all sincerity; I warn you against some thoughts that could cross your minds; frankness makes it incumbent upon me to tell you the following:

First, I have not come here for a separate agreement between Egypt and Israel. This is not part of the policy of Egypt. The problem is not that of Egypt and Israel. Any separate peace between Egypt and Israel, or between any Arab confrontation state and Israel, will not bring permanent peace based on justice in the entire region. Rather, even if peace between all the confrontation states and Israel were achieved, in the absence of a just solution to the Palestinian problem, never will there be that durable and just peace upon which the entire world insists today.

Second, I have not come to you to seek a partial peace, namely to terminate the state of belligerency at this stage, and put off the entire problem to a subsequent stage. This is not the radical solution that would steer us to permanent peace.

Equally, I have not come to you for a third disengagement agreement in Sinai, or in the Golan and the West Bank, for this would mean that we are merely delaying the ignition of the fuse. It would mean that we are lacking the courage to confront peace, that we are too weak to shoulder the burdens and responsibilities of a durable peace based on justice.

I have come to you so that together we might build a durable peace based on justice, to avoid the shedding of one single drop of blood from an Arab or an Israeli. It is for this reason that I have proclaimed my readiness to go to the farthest corner of the world.

Here, I would go back to the answer to the big question: How can we achieve a durable peace based on justice?

In my opinion, and I declare it to the whole world from this forum, the answer is neither difficult nor impossible, despite long years of feud, blood vengeance, spite and hatred, and breeding generations on concepts of total rift and deep-rooted animosity. The answer is not difficult, nor is it impossible, if we sincerely and faithfully follow a straight line.

You want to live with us in this part of the world. In all sincerity, I tell you, we welcome you among us, with full security and safety. This, in itself, is a tremendous turning point: one of the landmarks of a decisive historical change.

We used to reject you. We had our reasons and our claims, yes. We used to brand you as "so-called" Israel, yes. We were together in international conferences and organizations and our representatives did not, and still do not, exchange greetings, yes. This has happened and is still happening.

It is also true that we used to set, as a precondition for any negotiations with you, a mediator who would meet separately with each party. Through this procedure, the talks of the first and second disengagement agreements took place.

Our delegates met in the first Geneva Conference without exchanging a direct word. Yes, this has happened.

Yet, today I tell you, and declare it to the whole world, that we accept to live with you in permanent peace based on justice. We do not want to encircle you or be encircled ourselves by destructive missiles ready for launching, nor by the shells of grudges and hatred. I have announced on more than one occasion that Israel has become a *fait accompli* recognized by the world and that the two superpowers have undertaken the responsibility of its security and the defense of its existence.

As we really and truly seek peace, we really and truly welcome you to live among us in peace and security.

There was a huge wall between us which you tried to build up over a quarter of a century, but it was destroyed in 1973. It was a wall of a continuously inflammable and escalating psychological warfare. It was a wall of fear of the force that could sweep the entire Arab nation. It was a wall of propaganda, that we were a nation reduced to a motionless corpse. Rather, some of you had gone as far as to say that, even after fifty years, the Arabs would not regain any strength. It was a wall that threatened always with the long arm that could reach and strike anywhere. It was a wall that warned us against extermination and annihilation if we tried to use our legitimate right to liberate the occupied territories. Together we have to admit that that wall fell and collapsed in 1973.

Yet, there remained another wall. This wall constitutes a psychological barrier between us. A barrier of suspicion. A barrier of rejection. A barrier of fear of deception. A barrier of hallucinations around any action, deed, or decision. A barrier of cautious and erroneous interpretations of all and every event or statement. It is this psychological barrier which I described in official statements as representing 70 percent of the whole problem.

Today through my visit to you, I ask you, Why don't we stretch out our hands with faith and sincerity so that, together, we might destroy this barrier? Why shouldn't our and your will meet with faith and sincerity, so that together we might remove all suspicion of fear, betrayal and ill intentions? Why don't we stand together with the bravery of men and the boldness of heroes who dedicate themselves to a sublime objective? Why don't we stand together with the same courage and boldness to erect a huge edifice of peace that builds and does not destroy? An edifice that is a beacon for generations to come—the human message for construction, development and the dignity of man? Why should we bequeath to the coming generations the plight of bloodshed, death, orphans, widowhood, family disintegration, and the wailing of victims?

Why don't we believe in the wisdom of God as conveyed to us by the Proverbs of Solomon:

"Deceit is in the heart of them that imagine evil; but to the counsellors of peace is joy. Better is a dry morsel, and quietness therewith, than a house full of sacrifices with strife."

Why don't we repeat together from the Psalms of
David:

"Hear the voice of my supplications, when I cry unto
thee, when I lift up my hands toward the holy oracle.
Draw me not away with the wicked, and with the
workers of iniquity, which speak peace to their neigh-
bors, but mischief is in their hearts. Give them according
to their deeds, and according to the wickedness of their
endeavors."

To tell you the truth, peace cannot be worth its name
unless it is based on justice, and not on the occupation of
the land of others. It would not be appropriate for you to
demand for yourselves what you deny others. With all
frankness, and with the spirit that has prompted me to
come to you today, I tell you: You have to give up, once
and for all, the dreams of conquest, and give up the
belief that force is the best method for dealing with the
Arabs. You should clearly understand and assimilate the
lesson of confrontation between you and us.

Expansion does not pay. To speak frankly, our land
does not yield itself to bargaining. It is not even open to
argument. To us, the national soil is equal to the holy
valley where God Almighty spoke to Moses—peace be
upon him. None of us can, or accept to, cede one inch of
it, nor accept the principle of debating or bargaining
over it.

I sincerely tell you that before us today lies the
appropriate chance for peace, if we are really serious in
our endeavors for peace. It is a chance that time cannot
afford once again. It is a chance that, if lost or wasted,
the plotter against it will bear the curse of humanity and
the curse of history.

What is peace for Israel? It means that Israel lives in
the region with her Arab neighbors, in security and

safety. To such logic, I say yes. It means that Israel lives within her borders, secure against any aggression. To such logic, I say yes. It means that Israel obtains all kinds of guarantees that ensure those two factors. To this demand, I say yes. More than that: We declare that we accept all the international guarantees you envisage and accept. We declare that we accept all the guarantees you want from the two superpowers or from either of them, or from the Big Five, or some of them.

Once again, I declare clearly and unequivocally that we agree to any guarantees you accept because, in return, we shall obtain the same guarantees.

In short, then, when we ask what is peace for Israel, the answer would be: It is that Israel live within her borders with her Arab neighbors, in safety and security within the framework of all the guarantees she accepts and which are offered to the other party. But how can this be achieved? How can we reach this conclusion which would lead us to permanent peace based on justice?

There are facts that should be faced with all courage and clarity. There are Arab territories which Israel has occupied by armed force. We insist on complete withdrawal from these territories, including Arab Jerusalem.

I have come to Jerusalem, as the City of Peace, which will always remain as a living embodiment of coexistence among believers of the three religions. It is inadmissible that anyone should conceive the special status of the City of Jerusalem within the framework of annexation or expansionism, but it should be a free and open city for all believers.

Above all, the city should not be severed from those who have made it their abode for centuries. Instead of awakening the prejudices of the Crusaders, we should revive the spirit of Omar ibn el-Khattab and Saladdin, namely the spirit of tolerance and respect for rights. The holy shrines of Islam and Christianity are not only places of worship, but a living testimony of our uninterrupted presence here politically, spiritually, and intellectually. Let us make no mistake about the importance and reverence we Christians and Muslims attach to Jerusalem.

Let me tell you, without the slightest hesitation, that I did not come to you under this dome to make a request that your troops evacuate the occupied territories. Complete withdrawal from the Arab territories occupied in 1967 is a logical and undisputed fact. Nobody should plead for that. Any talk about permanent peace based on justice, and any move to ensure our coexistence in peace and security in this part of the world, would become meaningless, while you occupy Arab territories by force of arms. For there is no peace that could be in consonance with, or be built on, the occupation of the land of others. Otherwise, it would not be a serious peace.

Yes, this is a foregone conclusion which is not open to discussion or debate—if intentions are sincere and if endeavors to establish a just and durable peace for ours and the generations to come are genuine.

As for the Palestinians' cause, nobody could deny that it is the crux of the entire problem. Nobody in the world could accept, today, slogans propagated here in Israel, ignoring the existence of the Palestinian people, and questioning their whereabouts. The cause of the Palestinian people and their legitimate rights are no longer ignored or denied today by anybody. Rather, nobody who has the ability of judgment can deny or ignore it.

It is an acknowledged fact received by the world community, both in the East and in the West, with support and recognition in international documents and official statements. It is of no use to anybody to turn deaf ears to its resounding voice which is being heard day and night, or to overlook its historical reality. Even the United States, your first ally—which is absolutely committed to safeguard Israel's security and existence, and which offered and still offers Israel every moral, material and military support—I say, even the United States has opted to face up to reality and facts and admit that the Palestinian people are entitled to legitimate rights and that the Palestinian problem is the core and essence of the conflict and that, so long as it continues to be unresolved, the conflict will continue to aggravate, reaching new dimensions. In all sincerity, I tell you that there can be no peace without the Palestinians. It is a grave error of unpredictable consequences to overlook or brush aside this cause.

I shall not indulge in past events since the Balfour Declaration sixty years ago. You are well acquainted with the relevant facts. If you have found the legal and moral justification to set up a national home on a land that did not all belong to you, it is incumbent upon you to show understanding of the insistence of the people of Palestine on establishing, once again [*sic*], a state on their land. When some extremists ask the Palestinians to give up this sublime objective, this, in fact, means asking them to renounce their identity and every hope for the future.

I hail the Israeli voices that called for the recognition of the Palestinian people's rights to achieve and safe-guard peace. Here I tell you, ladies and gentlemen, that it is no use to refrain from recognizing the Palestinian people and their rights to statehood and rights of return.

We, the Arabs, have faced this experience before, with you and with the reality of Israeli existence. The struggle took us from war to war, from victims to more victims, until you and we have today reached the edge of a horrifying abyss and a terrifying disaster, unless together we seize the opportunity today of a durable peace based on justice.

You have to face reality bravely as I have done. There can never be any solution to a problem by evading it or turning a deaf ear to it. Peace cannot last if attempts are made to impose fantasy concepts on which the world has turned its back and announced its unanimous call for the respect of rights and facts. There is no need to enter a vicious circle as to Palestinian rights. It is useless to create obstacles. Otherwise the march of peace will be impeded or peace will be blown up.

As I have told you, there is no happiness to the detriment of others. Direct confrontation and straight-forwardness are the short-cut and the most successful way to reach a clear objective. Direct confrontation concerning the Palestinian problem, and tackling it in one single language with a view to achieving a durable and just peace, lie in the establishment of their state. With all the guarantees you demand, there should be no fear of a newly born state that needs the assistance of all countries of the world. When the bells of peace ring, there will be no hands to beat the drums of war. Even if they existed, they would be soundless.

Conceive with me a peace agreement in Geneva that we would herald to a world thirsty for peace, a peace agreement based on the following points:

First, ending the Israeli occupation of the Arab territories occupied in 1967.

Second, achievement of the fundamental rights of the Palestinian people and their right to self-determination, including their right to establish their own state.

Third, the right of all states in the area to live in peace within their boundaries, which will be secure and guaranteed through procedures to be agreed upon, which provide appropriate security to international boundaries, in addition to appropriate international guarantees.

Fourth, commitment of all states in the region to administer the relations among them in accordance with the objectives and principles of the United Nations Charter, particularly the principles concerning the non-resort to force and the resolution of differences among them by peaceful means.

Fifth, ending the state of belligerency in the region.

Ladies and gentlemen, peace is not the mere endorsement of written lines; rather, it is a rewriting of history. Peace is not a game of calling for peace to defend certain whims or hide certain ambitions. Peace is a giant struggle against all and every ambition and whim. Perhaps the examples taken from ancient and modern history teach us all that missiles, warships, and nuclear weapons cannot establish security. Rather, they destroy what peace and security build. For the sake of our peoples, and for the sake of the civilizations made by man, we have to defend man everywhere against the rule of the force of arms, so that we may endow the rule of humanity with all the power of the values and principles that promote the sublime position of mankind.

Allow me to address my call from this rostrum to the people of Israel. I address myself with true and sincere words to every man, woman, and child in Israel.

From the Egyptian people who bless this sacred mission of peace, I convey to you the message of peace, the message of the Egyptian people who do not know fanaticism, and whose sons, Muslims, Christians, and Jews, live together in a spirit of cordiality, love, and tolerance. This is Egypt whose people have entrusted me with that sacred message, the message of security, safety, and peace. To every man, woman and child in Israel, I say: Encourage your leadership to struggle for peace. Let all endeavors be channeled toward building a huge edifice for peace, instead of strongholds and hideouts defended by destructive rockets. Introduce to the entire world the image of the new man in this area, so that he might set an example to the man of our age, the man of peace everywhere.

Be the heralds to your sons. Tell them that past wars were the last of wars and the end of sorrows. Tell them that we are in for a new beginning to a new life—the life of love, prosperity, freedom, and peace.

You, bewailing mother; you, widowed wife; you, the son who lost a brother or a father; you, all victims of wars: Fill the earth and space with recitals of peace. Fill bosoms and hearts with the aspirations of peace. Turn the song into a reality that blossoms and lives. Make hope a code of conduct and endeavor. The will of peoples is part of the will of God.

Ladies and gentlemen, before I came to this place, with every beat of my heart and with every sentiment, I prayed to God Almighty, while performing the Curban Bairam prayers, and while visiting the Holy Sepulchre, to give me strength and to confirm my belief that this visit may achieve the objectives I look forward to, for a happy present and a happier future.

I have chosen to set aside all precedents and traditions known by warring countries, in spite of the fact that occupation of the Arab territories is still there. Rather, the declaration of my readiness to proceed to Israel came as a great surprise that stirred many feelings and astounded many minds. Some opinions even doubted its intent. Despite that, the decision was inspired by all the clarity and purity of belief, and with all the true expression of my people's will and intentions.

And I have chosen this difficult road, which is considered in the opinion of many the most difficult road. I have chosen to come to you with an open heart and an open mind. I have chosen to give this great impetus to all international efforts exerted for peace. I have chosen to present to you, and in your own home, the realities devoid of any schemes or whims, not to manoeuvre or to win a round, but for us to win together, the most dangerous of rounds and battles in modern history: the battle of permanent peace based on justice.

It is not my battle alone, nor is it the battle of the leadership in Israel alone. It is the battle of all and every citizen in all our territories whose right it is to live in peace. It is the commitment of conscience and responsibility in the hearts of millions.

When I put forward this initiative, many asked what is it that I conceived as possible to achieve during this visit, and what my expectations were. And, as I answered the questioners, I announce before you that I have not thought of carrying out this initiative from the concept of what could be achieved during this visit, but I have come here to deliver a message. I have delivered the message, and may God be my witness.

I repeat with Zechariah, *"Love right and justice."*

I quote the following verses from the holy Qur'an:

"We believe in God and in what has been revealed to us and what was revealed to Abraham, Ishmael, Isaac, Jacob, and the tribes and in the books given to Moses, Jesus, and the prophets from their Lord. We make no distinction between one and another among them, and to God we submit."

Appendix B

Prime Minister Menachem Begin
Address to the Israeli Knesset
November 20, 1977

M r. Speaker, Mr. President of the State of Israel, Mr. President of the Arab Republic of Egypt, ladies and gentlemen, members of the Knesset: We send our greetings to the president, to all the people of the Islamic religion in our country, and wherever they may be, on this occasion of the feast of the festival of the sacrifice 'Id al-Adha. This feast reminds us of the binding of Isaac. This was the way in which the Creator of the World tested our forefather, Abraham, our common forefather, to test his faith, and Abraham passed this test. However, from the moral aspect and the advancement of humanity, it was forbidden to sacrifice human beings. Our two peoples in their ancient traditions know and taught what the Lord, blessed be He, taught while peoples around us still sacrificed human beings to their gods. Thus, we contributed, the people of Israel and the Arab people, to the progress of mankind, and thus we are continuing to contribute to human culture to this day.

I greet and welcome the president of Egypt for coming to our country and on his participating in the Knesset session. The flight time between Cairo and Jerusalem is short, but the distance between Cairo and Jerusalem was until last night almost endless. President Sadat crossed this distance courageously. We, the Jews, know how to appreciate such courage, and we know how to appreciate it in our guest, because it is with courage that we are here, and this is how we continue to exist, and we shall continue to exist.

Mr. Speaker, this small nation, the remaining refuge of the Jewish people who returned to their historic homeland, has always wanted peace, and since the dawn of our independence, on May 14, 1948, 5 Iyar Tashah, in the declaration of independence in the founding scroll of our national freedom, David Ben Gurion said, "We extend a hand of peace and neighborliness to all the neighboring countries and their peoples. We call upon them to cooperate, to help each other, with the Hebrew people independent in their own country. One year earlier, even from the underground, when we were in the midst of the fateful struggle for the liberation of the country and the redemption of the people, we called on our neighbors in these terms: In this country we will live together and we will advance together and we will live lives of freedom and happiness. Our Arab neighbors, do not reject the hand stretched out to you in peace."

But it is my bounden duty, Mr. Speaker, and not only my right, not to pass over the truth that our hand outstretched for peace was not grasped and one day after we had renewed our independence, as was our right, our eternal right, which cannot be disputed, we were attacked on three fronts, and we stood almost without arms, the few against many, the weak against the strong, while an attempt was made, one day after the declaration of independence, to strangle it at birth, to put an end to the last hope of the Jewish people, the yearning renewed after the years of destruction and holocaust. No, we did not believe in might and we have never based our attitude toward the Arab people on might. Quite the contrary, force was used against us. Over all the years of this generation we have never stopped being attacked by

might, by the strong arm stretched out to exterminate our
people, to destroy our independence, to deny our rights.
We defended ourselves, it is true. We defended our
rights, our existence, our honor, our women, and our
children against these repeated and recurring attempts to
crush us through the force of arms, and not only on one
front. That, too, is true. With the help of God Almighty,
we overcame the forces of aggression, and we have
guaranteed existence for our nation. Not only for this
generation, but for the coming generations, too. We do
not believe in might. We believe in right, only in right.
And therefore our aspiration, from the bottom of our
hearts, has always been, to this very day, for peace.

Mr. President, Mr. President of Egypt, the commanders of all the underground Hebrew fighting organizations are sitting in this democratic house. They had to
conduct a campaign of the few against the many, against
a huge, a world power. Sitting here are the veteran
commanders and captains who had to go forth into battle
because it was forced upon them, and forward to victory,
which was unavoidable because they were defending
their rights. They belong to different parties. They have
different views, but I am sure, Mr. President, that I am
expressing the views of everyone, with no exceptions,
that we have one aspiration in our hearts, one desire in
our souls, and all of us are united in all these aspirations
and desires—to bring peace, peace for our nation, which
has not known peace for even one day since we started
returning to Zion, and peace for our neighbors, whom
we wish all the best, and we believe that if we make
peace, real peace, we will be able to help our neighbors,
in all walks of life, and a new era will open in the
Middle East, an era of blossoming and growth,

development and expansion of the economy, its growth as it was in the past.

Therefore, permit me today to set forth the peace program as we understand it. We want full, real peace with complete reconciliation between the Jewish and the Arab peoples. I do not wish to dwell on the memories of the past, but there have been wars; there has been blood spilled; wonderful young people have been killed on both sides. We will live all our life with the memories of our heroes who gave their lives so this day would arrive, this day, too, would come, and we respect the bravery of a rival and we honor all the members of the younger generation among the Arab people who also fell.

I do not wish to dwell on memories of the past, although they be bitter memories. We will bury them; we will worry about the future, about our people, our children, our joint and common future. For it is true indeed that we will have to live in this area, all of us together will live here, for generations upon generations: The great Arab people in their various states and countries, and the Jewish people in their country, Eretz Yisrael. Therefore, we must determine what peace means.

Let us conduct negotiations, Mr. President, as free negotiating partners for a peace treaty, and, with the aid of the Lord, we fully believe the day will come when we can sign it with mutual respect, and we will then know that the era of wars is over, that hands have been extended between friends, that each has shaken the hand of his brother and the future will be shining for all the peoples of this area. The beginning of wisdom in a peace treaty is the abolition of the state of war. I agree, Mr. President, that you did not come here, we did not invite you to our country in order, as has been said in recent days, to divide the Arab peoples. Somebody quoted an ancient Roman, saying: Divide and rule. Israel does not want to rule and therefore does not need to divide. We want peace with all our neighbors: with Egypt, with Jordan, with Syria, and with Lebanon. We would like to negotiate peace treaties.

And there is no need to distinguish between a peace treaty and an abolition of the state of war. Quite the contrary, we are not proposing this nor are we asking for it. The first clause of a peace treaty is cessation of the state of war forever. We want to establish normal relations between us, as they exist between all nations, even after wars. We have learned from history, Mr. President, that war is avoidable, peace is unavoidable. Many nations have waged war among themselves, and sometimes they used the tragic term "perennial enemy." There are no perennial enemies. And after all the wars the inevitable comes—peace. And so we want to establish, in a peace treaty, diplomatic relations as is the custom among civilized nations.

Today two flags are flying over Jerusalem: the Egyptian flag and the Israeli flag. And we saw together, Mr. President, little children waving both the flags. Let us sign a peace treaty and let us establish this situation forever, both in Jerusalem and in Cairo, and I hope the day will come when the Egyptian children wave the Israeli flag and the Egyptian flag, just as the children of Israel waved both these flags in Jerusalem.

And you, Mr. President, will have a loyal ambassador in Jerusalem, and we will have an ambassador in Cairo. And even if differences of opinion arise between us, we will clarify them like civilized peoples through our authorized envoys.

We are proposing economic cooperation for the development of our countries. These are wonderful countries in the Middle East. The Lord created it thus: oases in the desert, but there are deserts as well and we can make them flourish. Let us cooperate in this field. Let us develop our countries. Let us eliminate poverty, hunger, the lack of shelter. Let us raise our peoples to the level of developed countries and let them not call us "developing countries."

And with all due respect, I am willing to confirm the words of his majesty the king of Morocco, who said—in public too—that if peace arises in the Middle East, the combination of Arab genius and Jewish genius together can turn this area into a paradise on earth.

Let us open our countries to free traffic. You come to our country and we will visit yours. I am ready to announce, Mr. Speaker, this day that our country is open to the citizens of Egypt and I make no conditions on our part. I think it is only proper and just that there should be a joint announcement on this matter. But, just as there are Egyptian flags in our streets, and there is also an honored delegation from Egypt in our capital and in our country, let the number of visitors increase: Our border will be open to you, and also all the other borders.

And as I pointed out, we want this in the South and in the North and in the East. And so I am renewing my invitation to the president of Syria to follow in your footsteps, Mr. President, and come to us to open negotiations for achieving peace between Israel and Syria and to sign a peace treaty between us. I am sorry to say that there is no justification for the mourning they have declared beyond our northern border. Quite the contrary, such visits, such links, such clarifications can and must be days of joy, days of lifting spirits for all the peoples. I invite King Hussein to come to us to discuss all the problems which need to be discussed between us. Also genuine representatives of the Arabs of Eretz Yisrael, I invite them to come and hold talks with us to clarify our common future, to guarantee the freedom of man, social justice, peace, mutual respect. And if they invite us to go to their capitals, we will accept their invitations. If they invite us to open negotiations in Damascus, in Amman, or in Beirut, we will go to those capitals in order to hold negotiations with them there. We do not want to divide. We want real peace with all our neighbors, to be expressed in peace treaties whose contents I have already made clear.

Mr. Speaker, it is my duty today to tell our guest and the peoples watching us and listening to our words about the link between our people and this country. The president recalled the Balfour Declaration. No, sir, we did not take over any strange land; we returned to our homeland. The link between our people and this country is eternal. It arose in the earliest days of the history of humanity and has never been disrupted. In this country we developed our civilization, we had our prophets here, and their sacred words stand to this day. Here the kings of Judah and Israel knelt before their God. This is where we became a people; here we established our kingdom. And when we were expelled from our land because of force which was used against us, the farther we went from our land, we never forgot this country for even a single day. We prayed for it, we longed for it, we believed in our return to it from the day the words were spoken: *When the Lord restores the fortunes of Zion, we will be like dreamers. Our mouths will be filled with laughter, and our tongues will speak with shouts of joy.* These verses apply to all our exiles and all our sufferings, giving the consolation that the return to Zion would come.

This, our right, was recognized. The Balfour Declaration was included in the mandate laid down by the nations of the world, including the United States, and the preface to this recognized international document says, "Whereas recognition has the Bible given to the historical connection of the Jewish people with Palestine and to the grounds for reconstituting their national home in that country"—the historic connection between the Jewish people and Palestine—or, in Hebrew, Eretz Yisrael, was given reconfirmation—reconfirmation—as the national homeland in that country, that is, in Eretz Yisrael.

In 1919 we also won recognition of this right by the spokesman of the Arab people and the agreement of January 3, 1919, which was signed by Emir Faysal and Chaim Weizmann. It reads, "Mindful of the racial kinship and ancient bonds existing between the Arabs and the Jewish people and realizing that the surest means of working out the consummation of the national aspirations in the closest possible collaboration in the development of the Arab State and of Palestine." And afterward come all the clauses about cooperation between the Arab State and Eretz Yisrael. This is our right. The existence—truthful existence.

What happened to us when our homeland was taken from us? I accompanied you this morning, Mr. President, to Yad Vashem. With your own eyes you saw the fate of our people when this homeland was taken from it. It cannot be told. Both of us agreed, Mr. President, that anyone who has not seen with his own eyes everything there is in Yad Vashem cannot understand what happened to this people when it was without a homeland, when its own homeland was taken from it. And both of us read a document dated January 30, 1939, where the word "Vernichtung"—annihilation—appears. If war breaks out, the Jewish race in Europe will be exterminated. Then, too, we were told that we should not pay attention to the racists. The whole world heard. Nobody came to save us. Not during the nine fateful, decisive months after the announcement was made, the likes of which had not been seen since the Lord created man and man created the Devil.

And during those six years, too, when millions of our people, among them one and a half million of the little children of Israel who were burned on all the strange beds, nobody came to save them, not from the East nor from the West. And because of this, we took a solemn oath, this entire generation, the generation of extermination and revival, that we would never again put our people in danger, that we would never again put our women and our children, whom it is our duty to defend—if there is a need for this, even at the cost of our lives—in the hell of the exterminating fire of an enemy. Since then, it has been our duty for generations to come to remember that certain things said about our people must be taken with complete seriousness. And we must not, heaven forbid, for the sake of the future of our people, take any advice whatsoever against taking these things seriously.

President Sadat knows, and he knew from us before he came to Jerusalem, that we have a different position from his with regard to the permanent borders between us and our neighbors. However, I say to the president of Egypt and to all our neighbors: Do not say, "There is not negotiation, there will not be negotiations about any particular issue." I propose, with the agreement of the

decisive majority of this parliament, that everything be
open to negotiation. Anyone who says, with reference to
relations between the Arab people, or the Arab peoples
around us, and the State of Israel, that there are things
which should be omitted from negotiations, is taking
upon himself a grave responsibility: Everything can be
negotiated.

No side will say the contrary. No side will present
prior conditions. We will conduct the negotiations
honorably. If there are differences of opinion between
us, this is not unusual. Anyone who has studied the
histories of wars and the signing of peace treaties knows
that all negotiations over a peace treaty began with
differences of opinion between the sides. And in the
course of the negotiations they reach an agreement that
permits the signing of peace treaties and agreements.
And this is the road which we propose to take.

And we will conduct the negotiations as equals.
There are no vanquished and there are no victors. All the
peoples of the area are equal and all of them should treat
each other with due respect. In this spirit of openness, of
willingness to listen to each other, to hear the facts and
the reasoning and the explanations, accepting all the
experience of human persuasion, let us conduct the
negotiations as I have asked and am proposing, open
them and carry them out, carry them on constantly until
we reach the longed-for hour of the signing of a peace
treaty between us.

We are not only ready to sit with the representatives
of Egypt, and also with the representatives of Jordan and
Syria and Lebanon, if they are ready; we are prepared to
sit together at a peace conference in Geneva. We
propose that the Geneva conference be renewed, on the
basis of the two Security Council resolutions: 242 and

338. If there are problems between us by convening the Geneva conference, we will be able to clarify them. And if the president of Egypt wants to continue clarifying them in Cairo, I am for it. If in a neutral place, there is no objection. Let us clarify anywhere, even before the Geneva conference convenes, the problems which should be clarified before it is convened. And our eyes will be open and our ears will listen to all proposals.

Permit me to say a word about Jerusalem. Mr. President, you prayed today in the house of prayer sacred to the Islamic religion, and from there you went to the Church of the Holy Sepulchre. You realized, as those coming from all over the world have realized, that ever since this city was unified, there has been completely free access, without interference and without any obstacle, for the members of every religion to the places sacred to them. This positive phenomenon did not exist for nineteen years. It has existed for about eleven years, and we can promise the Muslim world and the Christian world, all the peoples, that there will always be free access to the sacred places of every religion. We will defend this right to free access, for we believe in it. We believe in equal rights for all men and citizens and respect for every faith.

Mr. Speaker, this is a special day for our legislative chamber, and certainly this day will be remembered for many years in the history of our nation, and perhaps also in the history of the Egyptian nation, maybe in the history of all nations. And this day, with your agreement, ladies and gentlemen, members of the Knesset, let us pray that the God of our fathers, our common fathers, will give us the wisdom needed to overcome difficulties and obstacles, calumnies and slander, incitement and attacks. And with the help of God, may we arrive at the longed-for day for which all our people pray—peace. For it is indeed true that the sweet singer of Israel [King David] said: "Righteousness and peace will kiss each other," and the Prophet Zachariah said: "Love, truth and peace."

Contributors

Jon B. Alterman is a historian and a Soref research fellow at the Washington Institute.

Eliahu Ben Elissar is the ambassador of Israel to the United States. A senior Likud official since 1970, he has served as Israel's first ambassador to Egypt, a member of Israel's delegation to the Madrid Peace Conference, and chairman of the Knesset Foreign Affairs and Defense Committee.

Wat Cluverius is director general of the Multinational Force and Observers, an international organization operating in the Sinai Peninsula that monitors the security provisions of the 1979 peace treaty between Egypt and Israel. He previously served as U.S. ambassador to Bahrain, U.S. consul general in Jerusalem, and senior adviser to the secretary of state for Middle East peace.

Hermann Frederick Eilts was U.S. ambassador to Egypt and Saudi Arabia. After his retirement from the foreign service, he served for many years as Distinguished University Professor of international relations at Boston University.

Ahmed Fakhr retired with the rank of major general from the Egyptian armed forces. He is the founder of the National Center for Middle Eastern Studies in Cairo.

Saad Eddin Ibrahim, a former visiting fellow at The Washington Institute, is a professor of political sociology at the American University in Cairo and chairman of the board of the Ibn Khaldoun Center for Development Studies.

Martin Indyk, founding executive director of The Washington Institute, is assistant secretary of state for Near Eastern affairs. He previously served as senior director of Near East and South Asian affairs at the National Security Council and as U.S. ambassador to Israel.

Samuel Lewis was counselor to The Washington Institute until January 1998 and currently serves as a member of its Board of Advisors. He served as director of the Department of State's Policy Planning Staff during Bill Clinton's first term and as U.S. ambassador to Israel under Presidents Jimmy Carter and Ronald Reagan. From 1987 to 1993, he was the president of the United States Institute of Peace.

Ahmed Maher el-Sayed is the ambassador of Egypt to the United States. He was director of the policy planning department in the Egyptian Ministry of Foreign Affairs and participated in the Camp David peace negotiations and the Taba negotiations between Egypt and Israel.

Robert Pelletreau served as assistant secretary of state for Near East affairs until January 1997. Prior to that, he was the U.S. ambassador to Egypt, Tunisia, and Bahrain. On leaving government, he joined the international law firm of Afridi & Angell.

Kenneth Pollack, a research fellow at The Washington Institute, has served as a Persian Gulf military analyst at the Central Intelligence Agency and in the Near East and

South Asia directorate at the National Security Council. He is currently working on a study of Egyptian national security and the Egyptian armed forces.

Peter Rodman is the director of National Security Programs at the Nixon Center for Peace and Freedom and a senior editor of the *National Review*. He formerly served as deputy national security adviser, director of the Department of State's Policy Planning Staff, and as a special assistant to Henry Kissinger on the NSC staff in the administrations of Richard Nixon and Gerald Ford.

Camelia Anwar Sadat is the daughter of the late peacemaker, Nobel laureate, and president of Egypt, Anwar Sadat. She is completing her doctorate in peace studies at Boston University under the supervision of Elie Wiesel.

Abdel Monem Said is the director of the al-Ahram Center for Political and Strategic Studies in Cairo. A participant in the "Copenhagen Process" of Arab and Israeli intellectuals committed to the peace process, he has written widely in Arabic and English on international relations, national security, and Egyptian affairs.

Robert Satloff is the executive director of The Washington Institute for Near East Policy. Among his publications is a Washington Institute Policy Paper, *Army and Politics in Mubarak's Egypt* (1988). In April 1997, he delivered testimony on U.S.–Egyptian relations before the House International Relations Committee.

Shimon Shamir was Israel's ambassador to Egypt and Jordan. He is the former director of the Israeli Academic Center in Cairo and has been a leader in promoting "people-to-people" contacts between Israeli and Egyptian intellectuals and political leaders.

Kenneth Stein is a historian and the director of the Middle East Research Program at Emory University. He is the co-author, with Samuel Lewis, of *Making Peace Among Arabs and Israelis: Lessons from Fifty Years of Negotiating Experience* (United States Institute of Peace, 1991).

Shibley Telhami holds the Anwar Sadat Chair for Population, Development, and Peace at the University of Maryland. He is the author of *Power and Leadership in International Bargaining: The Path to the Camp David Accords* (Columbia University Press, 1990).

Ehud Ya'ari, an associate of The Washington Institute, is the chief Middle East correspondent for Israel Television and, currently, its Washington correspondent. He is also a regular columnist for the *Jerusalem Report* and *Ma'ariv* newspaper. He is author of a Washington Institute Policy Paper, *Peace by Piece: A Decade of Egyptian Policy Toward Israel* (1989), and co-author, with Ze'ev Schiff, of *The Year of the Dove* (Bantam, 1979)

INSTITUTE STAFF